ANIMAL GUISING AND THE KENTISH HOODEN HORSE

AN EXHIBITION AT MAIDSTONE MUSEUM
8 FEBRUARY – 17 JUNE 2023

JAMES FROST

with contributions from Geoff Doel and Ben Jones ('George')

Animal Guising and the Kentish Hooden Horse
Written, compiled and edited by James Frost.
© James Frost, 2023 except where otherwise noted or evident from context.
Cover image: photograph (c.1910-1939) by Gordon Chase of 'Wingham' hooden horse, from Maylam Family Archives.

Every reasonable effort was made to track down the copyright holders for all content used in this publication. Please contact us if you become aware of any copyrighted material used inappropriately. Material believed to be out of copyright has been edited to correct obvious errors and conform to modern typographical conventions, while retaining the original text as far as possible. Original texts are often inconsistent in their spelling of molly/mollie or wagoner/waggoner, etc. so we have standardized on the former, but left the alternatives in place in some direct quotations.

All rights reserved. No part of this document may be reproduced, copied, distributed, transferred, modified, or transmitted, in any form or by any means, electronic or mechanical, including photocopying, recording, or by any information storage or retrieval system, without the prior written permission of the copyright owner; nor can it be circulated in any form of binding or cover other than that in which it is published and without similar conditions including this condition being imposed on a subsequent purchaser. In no event shall the author or publisher be liable for any damages caused in any way by use of this document.

Published by Ōzaru Books, an imprint of BJ Translations Ltd
Street Acre, St Nicholas-at-Wade, BIRCHINGTON, CT7 0NG, U.K.
https://ozaru.net/ozarubooks

This edition published 1 January 2023
ISBN: 978-1-915174-06-2

CONTENTS

List of Illustrations 1
Dedications 3
Foreword and Acknowledgements 5
The Kent Hooden Horse: An Introduction 7
What was Hoodening? 13

    What does 'hoodening' mean? 15
    Who were the hoodeners? 17
    What did they perform? 19
    Why did they do it? 24
    Summary 25

The Exhibits 29

    The Kentish Hoodening Tradition 31
    Reviving the Hooden Horse 51
    What is Autohoodening? 71
    The Northern Beasts 79
    Mari Lwyd of Wales 91
    Hobby Horses and Obby Osses 99
    Stag Guising 113
    What do animal disguises say about our relationship with animals? 124

My life as a hoodener 129
Appendix 1: Modern Hoodening Verses 135

    'The Hooden Horse' by Phil Martin 135
    'The Finest Hooden Horse' by Gail Duff (1998) 135
    'The Hooden Horse' by Gail Duff (11 November 2003) 136
    'The Wagoner's Tale' by Gail Duff (2017) 137
    'Being Horse' by Sonia Overall (2019) 138

Appendix 2: Modern Hoodening Plays 141

    St Nicholas-at-Wade with Sarre 1966 play 141

Whitstable Hoodening Play 145
Tonbridge Hooden Horse Play 153
Swale Hoodening Play 157
The Canterbury Hooden Horse 163
The Hoodening Play of Dover Tales... 165
Autohoodening 172

About the author... 177
Ōzaru Books 178

LIST OF ILLUSTRATIONS

1 'Dobbin' and Wagoner, St Nicholas-at-Wade Hoodeners (c.1921)..........................14
2 Symondsbury Mummers' 'Tommy' hobby horse, Dorset (pre-20th century)..........22
3 'Dobbin' of the St Nicholas-at-Wade Hoodeners (June 1905)................................32
4 'Dobbin', St Nicholas-at-Wade hooden horse (pre-20th century).............................33
5 'Dobbin' with the St Nicholas-at-Wade Hoodeners (June 1905).............................34
6 'Dobbin' with the St Nicholas-at-Wade Hoodeners (c.1919)...................................35
7 Chislet hooden horse (1906, repainted 2009)...37
8 Hooden horse found at Wingham (c.1900–1910)...38
9 'Wingham' hooden horse (c.1910-1939)..39
10 'Colt' hooden horse found at Wingham (c.1870–1880)..40
11 'Walmer Court' hooden horse (c.1850s)..41
12 'Walmer Court' Hoodeners (1907)..42
13 Walmer 'Colt' hooden horse (1955)...43
14 Robert John Thomas Skardon and the Deal hooden horse (1909)............................44
15 Instruments of the North Deal Band and horse whip..45
16 Julia Small's 'Hengist' (c.1970s)..46
17 Deal Hoodeners' Horse (1997)...47
18 'Satan' hooden horse (pre-20th century)...48
19 The 'Brown Horse' at Folkestone International Folk Festival (1985)......................52
20 The 'Brown Horse' and John Field in morris dancing kit at the Queen's Coronation celebrations (1953)..53
21 Barnett Field and the 'Brown Horse'..53
22 Barnett and Olive Field's 'Brown Horse' (1953)..54
23 The Beckenham Morris Dancers with a hooden horse, fed by a fool (1950)...........55
24 Olive Field (centre) with the Handbell Hoodeners and 'Brown Horse', at Folkestone International Folklore Festival...56
25 East Kent Morris Men with 'Invicta' at Folkestone International Folklore Festival (late 1960s)...57
26 Hooden horse collection box, East Kent Morris (before 1964)................................58
27 The 'Giant Horse' at Folkestone International Folklore Festival (1971).................59
28 The 'Giant Horse' at Folkestone International Folklore Festival (1980s)................59
29 'Hooden Horse' pub sign, Wickhambreaux (1956)...60
30 Birchington Town Women's Guild hooden horse (1954)...61
31 Edward Coomber's hooden horse (early 1950s)..62
32 'Stinky', the Dead Horse Morris skull disguise (2003)...65
33 Jim 'the Ram' Bywater's Whitstable May Day hooden horse (1976, repainted 2005)...67
34 'Hobby' the horse, Broadstairs Folk Week..68
35 Alexis the Warehouse Scanner (2020)...72

36 Line Manager's costume (2020) 73
37 Line Manager's laptop (2020) 74
38 Captain Swing's costume (2020) 75
39 Captain Swing's computer bugs (2020) 76
40 Film still from *Autohoodening and the Rise of Captain Swing*, Post Workers Theatre and Infinite Opera (2021) 76
41 Skull horse from Richmond, Yorkshire (1956) 80
42 'Old Horse' skull disguise, retrieved from the pond at Hooten Pagnell Hall, Yorkshire (1880s) 81
43 Skull horse from Richmond, Yorkshire (c.1880) 82
44 'Lucky' the Wild Horse, Comberbach Mummers, Cheshire (1985) 86
45 'Old Tup', Handsworth, S. Yorkshire (c.1900) 88
46 The Comberbach Mummers' 'Tup', Cheshire (c.1985) 89
47 Ben Edge, *The Mari Lwyd* (2018) 92
48 Mari Lwyd with carved wooden head, Glamorgan, Wales (19th century) 93
49 Mari Lwyd, possibly from Merthyr Tydfil (1929–1935) 94
50 Mari Lwyd, Glamorgan, Wales (c.1920) 94
51 Ben Edge, *The Obby Oss of Padstow* (2018) 100
52 Blue Ribbon Oss and teaser, Padstow, Cornwall (May 1964) 101
53 May Day, Padstow (c.1835) – drawing reproduced in Thurston Peter's 'The Hobby Horse' (1913) 102
54 Obby Oss souvenir model, Padstow, Cornwall (2002) 103
55 'The Original Old 'Oss' poster, Padstow, Cornwall (2000) 104
56 Minehead Sailors' Horse (c.1948) 104
57 Ben Edge, *Hunting of the Earl of Rone* (2020) 105
58 Hunting the Earl of Rone hobby horse skirt, Combe Martin, Devon ... 106
59 Black Dog Oss, Devon (1993) 107
60 Bidford Morris Dancers hobby horse (c.1900) 108
61 Hobby horse detail from the 'Merry May' stained glass window, Betley Hall, Staffordshire (1621) 109
62 'Hob Nob', Salisbury, Wiltshire (c.1950) 110
63 Plough Monday hobby horse from Burringham, Lincolnshire (c.1920) 111
64 Ben Edge, *Abbots Bromley Horn Dance* (2018) 114
65 Abbots Bromley Horn Dancers (1963) 115
66 George Bradbury's replica of an Abbots Bromley Horn Dance antler head (c.1929–1930) 117
67 Abbots Bromley Horn Dancers, Staffordshire inc. hobby horse, Fool, Maid Marian and Robin Hood (c.1890) 118
68 Stag disguise marginalia in the *Romance of Alexander* (1338–1344) 121
69 Star Carr frontlets (c.9000 BCE) 123

DEDICATIONS

Aaron Janes (1974–2022), dearly missed on the Kentish folk scene. A talented musician and former member of the Whitstable Hoodeners, Dead Horse and Wantsum Morris.

Chris Smith (1941–2022), former landlord of the Gate Inn, Marshside, who helped foster a folk drama community there and who rescued an old hooden horse.

FOREWORD AND ACKNOWLEDGEMENTS

James Frost

This exhibition is about what hoodening was, what the hooden horse is, and how it can be seen in the national context of animal guising. Due to space and other constraints the exhibition focuses on animal guising in England and Wales exclusively. However, there are many analogous customs and animal disguises in Ireland, Newfoundland, Iceland, Continental Europe, Africa and elsewhere which are equally fascinating.

I first came across the hooden horse in Ronald Hutton's book *Stations of the Sun* (1996). I was intrigued by the 'Ancient Order of Hoodeners' that he mentions, but later discovered that they don't exist. Perhaps this was an off-hand joke by a hoodener when interviewed by Hutton in Whitstable.

I had been working as a puppeteer and street performer when, in 2004, I took part in the Whitstable May Day procession as a 'tourney' hobby horse with Oyster Morris. This prompted the organizer Dixie Lee to give me Jim 'the Ram' Bywater's Whitstable May Day hooden horse to perform the following year, and I have done so every year since. I made a new hooden horse for the first Sandwich Folk and Ale Festival in 2011 and it became the Canterbury Hoodeners' horse when I co-founded that group in 2016, with Geoff Doel's mentorship. Attending the annual hoodening meet (perhaps the closest thing to that 'Ancient Order'), my contacts in the hoodening community expanded. I realized I had enough research material and access to artefacts to approach Maidstone Museum for an exhibition. This was also a great opportunity to exhibit the two old hooden horses in their collection, usually hidden away in storage because of their delicate condition.

The exhibition showcases some thirty animal disguises of different kinds, including the oldest surviving hooden horses. There is also a petting area of modern beasts in the foyer for more haptic engagement with the artefacts.

A heartfelt thanks to everyone who has helped, given time, offered to perform, lent horses and dug out photographs for this landmark exhibition and publication.

Particular thanks to:

- The Arts Council, England
- National Lottery Heritage Fund
- Alex Gurr, Lyn Palmer and Pernille Richards of Maidstone Museum
- Maidstone Borough Council and Fremlin Walk
- Kathryn Reilly and Kathryn Penn-Simkins of Deal Museum

- Natasha Logan of the Horniman Museum
- Darran Cowd of Folkestone Museum
- Tiffany Hore, Nick Wall and Malcolm Barr-Hamilton of the Vaughan Williams Library at Cecil Sharp House
- Jennifer A. Cutting of the American Folklife Center, Library of Congress, Washington D.C.
- Dr Jody Joy, FSA, of the Museum of Archaeology and Anthropology, University of Cambridge
- Dr Sonia Overall of Canterbury Christ Church University
- Mark Norman of the Folklore Podcast
- Fred Mead
- Ben Edge
- Richard Maylam and Liz Hamilton
- Claire Louise Janes
- Hazel Tasker and Rosamund Horne
- Dixie Lee
- George Frampton
- Dr Geoff Doel
- Prof Ronald Hutton
- John Field
- David and Sarah Googe
- Clair and Carli of Lunatraktors
- Rosa Irwin Clark
- I.M.E (Invictus Mugistis Equinus) and Broadstairs Folk Week
- Ben Jones and the St Nicholas-at-Wade with Sarre Hoodeners
- Steve Grayland and the Deal Hoodeners
- Dominc Lucas and Dover Tales
- Gail Duff and Rabble Folk Theatre
- Mark Lawson and Alex Clifton-Fearnside of Whitstable Hoodeners and Dead Horse Morris
- Paula Jardine-Rose and the Wychling Hoodeners
- Harry Harrison and the Symondsbury Mummers
- Nicholas Mortimer, Dash Macdonald and Demitrios Kargotis of Post Workers Theatre
- and fellow Canterbury and Tonbridge hoodeners

THE KENT HOODEN HORSE: AN INTRODUCTION

Dr Geoff Doel

> 'My hide unto the huntsman, so freely I would give,
> My body to the fox dogs, I'd rather die than live.
> Although these gallant limbs have run so many miles,
> O'er hedges, ditches, brambles,
> And likewise gates and styles.
> Poor old horse!'
>
> 'Rise up old horse, and shine again!'
>
> (extracts from two 'Poor Old Horse' songs)

From the end of the eighteenth century, antiquarians began to take a greater interest in the traditional customs of the people and to document these in the increasing genre of magazine articles; some of these accounts were based on direct observation, others on hearsay or from earlier written accounts. Among them were many Christmas customs featuring groups of young men who toured from house to house or farm to farm with celebratory rituals such as mummers plays, sword dances, wassailing and animal disguise customs, varying according to locality. One of these was the East Kent custom of 'hoodening', an obscure term which may refer to the disguise of the 'hoodener' by being covered with sacking as he holds a carved horse's head. Typical of early references is a letter to the 'European Magazine' in 1807 which is helpfully detailed:

> At Ramsgate…I found they begin the festivities of Christmas by a curious procession: a party of young people procure the head of a dead horse, which is affixed to a pole about ten feet in length: a string is affixed to the lower jaw: a horse-cloth is also attached to the whole under which one of the party gets, and by frequently pulling the string, keeps up a loud snapping noise, and is accompanied by the rest of the party, grotesquely habited, with hand-bells: they thus process from house to house, ringing their bells, and singing carols and songs; they are commonly gratified with beer and cake, or perhaps with money. This is called provincially, a Hodening.

There may be some inaccuracies, such as the length of the pole, and subsequent descriptions of the hooden horse usually mention a wooden head. In Britain we find many other remnants of midwinter horse disguise customs, such as the Llair Bane of Ireland and Tommy the Pony of Dorset, both with wooden heads and the Welsh

Mari Lwyd, and the 'Poor Old Horses' of Lancashire, and the borders of Yorkshire, Derbyshire and Nottinghamshire and the Hallowe'en Cheshire traditions of the 'Wild Horse' using actual horse or donkey skulls. Of even wider currency are the 'Poor Old Horse Songs', which are more explicit about a death and resurrection aspect hinted at in the customs and perhaps analogous to the mumming and sword dance traditions, which are also connected to the survival of life at the midwinter crisis, as well as being seasonal fun. Some of the hooden horse descriptions mention the singing of carols and the ringing of handbells and the presence of musicians (usually with fiddle and fife in early accounts and concertina or accordion and tambourine in later ones), but the only specific hooden horse song to survive is the 'Blean Hoodening Song', which Percy Maylam mentions as being supplied by Thomas Culver of Broad Oak, near Sturry as being the 'stock song' of the Hoodeners in that area, the custom ceasing about 1870:

> Three jolly hoodening boys
> Lately come from town,
> Apples or for money
> We search the country round;
> Hats full, caps full,
> Half bushel baskets full-
> What you please to give us
> Happy we shall be.
> God bless every poor man
> Who's got an apple tree.

Although sung at Broad Oak by hoodeners, the subject matter is clearly apple wassailing and indeed the song was also found at Blean sung by groups of lads with no hooden horse, and at Eythorne in 1895 groups of lads calling themselves hoodeners (but without a horse) toured round shouting a Christmas refrain. Many accounts recorded by Maylam from the late nineteenth century indicate that the term 'hoodener' had taken on a wider context of Christmas entertainer in some areas.

The Mari Lwyd custom is the best-known horse disguise custom and possibly the oldest as it seems to be referred to in medieval Welsh poetry. Interestingly, the Mari is a mare, whereas most of the other cult horses seem to be stallions. The Mari seeks to enter farmhouses etc. by means of a rhyming battle in Welsh poetry (sometimes sung) and once inside it misbehaves, but is thought to bring a year's luck. As with the hooden horse there is a man/woman figure sweeping with besom broom, which has parallels in sixteenth and seventeenth century solstitial customs. The Symondsbury (Dorset) Tommy the Pony play has hints of divination, which links into traditional New Year beliefs.

The Canterbury solicitor and local historian Percy Maylam, who wrote the definitive book on the hooden horse in 1909, was one of a new band of much more accurate and detailed researchers of customs in the early twentieth century, interested in historical and social context and in the lives and occupations of the performers; he blends personal witnessing with meticulous research into documents and correspondence and first witnessed the custom as a young man in Thanet in the 1880s, which he vividly describes:

> Anyone who has spent a Christmas in a farm-house in Thanet – it has been my good fortune to spend five – will not forget Christmas Eve…The front door is flung open, and there they all are outside, the 'Waggoner' cracking his whip and leading the Horse … which assumes a most restive manner, champing his teeth, and rearing and plunging, and doing his best to unseat the 'Rider', who tries to mount him, while the 'Waggoner' shouts 'whoa!' and snatches at the bridle. 'Mollie' is there also! She is a lad dressed up in woman's clothes and vigorously sweeps the ground behind the horse with a birch broom. There are generally two or three other performers besides, who play the concertina, tambourine or instruments of that kind.

Percy Maylam's numerous accounts, including a letter of 1891 recounting the custom some forty-five years earlier from one who went the rounds with the hooden horse:

> It was always the custom on Christmas Eve with the male farm-servants in our parish of Hoath and neighbouring parishes of Herne and Chislet, to go round in the evening from house to house with the Hoodining Horse, which consisted of the imitation of a horse's head made of wood, life-size, fixed on a stick about the length of a broom handle: the lower jaw…was made to open with hinges, a hole was made through the roof of the mouth, then another by the forehead coming out by the throat, through this was passed a cord attached to the lower jaw, which when pulled…caused it to open; on the lower jaw large headed hob-nails were driven in to form the teeth…As soon as the doors were open the 'horse' would pull his string incessantly and the noise made can be better imagined than described…I have seen some of the wooden heads carved out quite hollow in the throat part, and two holes bored through the forehead to form the eyes. The lad who played the horse would hold a lighted candle in the hollow, and you can imagine how horrible it was to one who opened the door.

Percy Maylam visited, arranged photographs of, and described the survivals of the custom at St Nicholas-at-Wade, Walmer and Deal. The custom was in serious decline, with the Deal party, only having two members, but his intervention at St Nicholas brought back the recently discarded Molly. A letter sent to me in the 1980s from Naomi Wiffen, brought up in Deal shows the survival of the custom into the 1930s, probably the longest survival of the early sides:

> I remember as a child being taken out on Christmas Eve to the High Street in Deal where the shops would be open very late, and it was the only time Deal children were allowed out in the evening, as parents were very strict. As we would be looking at the lighted shops, and listening to the people selling their wares, a horrible growl, and a long horse's face would appear, resting on our shoulder and when one looked round, there would be a long row of teeth snapping at us with its wooden jaws. It was frightening for a child. Usually, there would be a man leading the horse, with a rope, and another covered over with sacks or blankets as the horse.

The Deal hooden horse custom probably survived long enough to almost overlap the first of the revivals inspired by Percy Maylam's book, at Balgowan School, Beckenham, although the Acol horse reappeared during the Second World War and the Ravensbourne Morris seems to have had a hooden horse from 1947. After a break of 40 years St Nicholas-at-Wade began a lively revival in the 1960s and is still going strong with an excellent website and archive organized by Ben Jones (see section **My Life as a Hoodener**); the revival at St Nicholas introduced a village play (different every year). A number of new sides and revivals sprang up in Thanet and elsewhere and the Broadstairs Folk Festival adopting the hooden horse as its symbol and morris sides such as The East Kent, Dead Horse and Hartley introduced hooden horses.

The first West Kent side appears to be the Ravensbourne Morris from 1947; I founded a Tonbridge side in 1981 with the idea of making the custom better known and we performed not only in the Tonbridge area at Christmas, but at the Kent County Show, stately homes, folk clubs the Broadstairs Folk Festival, for the Kent Archaeological Society and historical societies. Nick Miller of Hartley Morris (who feature a shorter version of our play) and myself wrote a play, strongly influenced by the Symondsbury and Antrobus traditions, featuring death and revival and divination to use by the Tonbridge Mummers & Hoodeners. South East Arts sponsored a book on the custom by my wife Fran and myself, which inspired the creation of a chain of hooden horse pubs, sadly no longer with us, and more hooden horse teams were revived or created, such as Deal, Dover, Whitstable, Sandgate, Sandling, Sandwich, Birchington and Chislet and variations of the play spread. There are no early references to plays in hooden horse accounts and it seems that the St Nicholas-at-Wade side were the first to use one. As Percy Maylam, the preserver of the hooden horse had strong Canterbury links, it's appropriate that the latest team is James Frost's Canterbury Hoodeners, which usually feature variants of the Tonbridge play at the Bell & Crown and is supported by Percy's great nephew Richard Maylam and myself as we both live locally now. Only 303 copies of Percy's book were printed originally, but Richard Maylam, Mick Lynn and myself have done a new edition for the History Press which has created some interest beyond the confines of Kent, including in universities.

A number of early hooden horses survive and are well documented in this excellent exhibition organized by James Frost, and I remember climbing into the attic at the Maidstone Museum over 30 years ago to find the two horses from Wingham via Wye College, which are in the exhibition, and photographing the then curator of the museum with his children holding them.

There is a possible link with the vibrant summer hobby horse tradition which is explored by Percy Maylam and by the current exhibition. Are they all remnants of early horse cults as Percy suggests, or independent traditions? The hooden horse remains a fascinating enigma in name and origin; the nineteenth-century accounts emphasize festive enjoyment and money and beer!

> 'We wish ye a merry Christmas
> And a happy New Year,
> A pocketful of money and
> A cellarful of beer.'
> (The Eythorne Hoodeners)

Bibliography

Cawte, E.C. (1978) *Ritual Animal Disguise: A Historical and Geographical Study of Animal Disguise in the British Isles*. Cambridge: D.S. Brewer.

Doel, F. and Doel, G. (1992) *Mumming, Howling and Hoodening: Midwinter Rituals in Sussex, Kent and Surrey*. Rainham: Meresborough Books.

Doel, F. and Doel, G. (2003) *Folklore of Kent*. Stroud: Tempus Publishing.

Doel, F. and Doel, G. (2023) *Horse Cults in the British Isles*. Fonthill.

Frampton, G. (2018) *Discordant Comicals: The Christmas Hoodeners of East Kent, Tradition and Revival*. 2nd edn. St Nicholas-at-Wade: Ozaru Books.

Hutton, R. (1996) *The Stations of the Sun: A History of the Ritual Year in Britain*. Oxford: Oxford University Press.

Maylam, R., Lynn, M. and Doel, G. (2009) *Percy Maylam's The Kent Hooden Horse*. Stroud: The History Press.

WHAT WAS HOODENING?

James Frost

1 'Dobbin' and Wagoner, St Nicholas-at-Wade Hoodeners (c.1921)
Credit: English Folk Dance and Song Society

Hoodening, as it was performed throughout the 19th and first half of the 20th century, was a Christmas house-calling custom based in East Kent.* This meant that a team would walk from one location to another, calling at houses, pubs and work places to perform. The Hooden Horse itself is a 'mast' disguise; a wooden head attached to a pole with the performer hidden beneath a cloth (**1**).

---

*The vast majority of material on this period of the custom was gathered in Percy Maylam's book *The Hooden Horse, an East Kent Christmas Custom* (1909). His material was reissued by Richard Maylam, Mick Lynn and Geoff Doel with additional material (2009). George Frampton expanded on Percy Maylam's research and extended the discussion to revival hoodening in his *Discordant Comicals: The Hooden Horse of East Kent* (2018). The subject has also interested folklorists and historians over the years, notably Violet Alford (1978), E.C. Cawte (1978) and Ronald Hutton (1996).

What does 'hoodening' mean?

The earliest known mention of hoodening is a definition in the *Alphabet of Kenticisms* compiled by Reverend Samuel Pegge, vicar of Godmersham, between 1735-6.

> Hooding [huod*ing] *sb.* a country masquerade at Christmas time, which in *Derb.* they call *guising* (I suppose a contraction of *dis-guising*), and in other places *mumming*. (p.82)

Notice first that the custom is here called 'Hooding' i.e. wearing a hood. Some sources in the 19th century use the spelling 'hodening'. The word 'hood' was occasionally spelt 'hode' until around this period; thus in Middle English texts we find 'Robin Hode'. Victorian antiquarians proposed a number of speculative etymologies for the word: a corruption of 'hobby', 'wooden' or the god 'Woden'. However, the root for the Middle English word 'hood/hode' is most likely from the Teutonic *hud,* meaning to 'cover'. We also derive another word from *hud*: to 'hide' (Skeat 1882). An interesting word of unknown origin is 'hodden', referring to a coarse woollen cloth. It seems likely that this word is also rooted in the word *hud*, as it is indeed a cloth covering. So, the word 'hooden' seems to well describe a horse disguise that covers one's head; this is consistent both in the Kentish dialect pronounciation and the etymology of the Middle English word 'hood'. Incidentally, there was once a 'Hoden Farm' in the village of Ash, near Sandwich, with deeds dating back to 1626. Hoodeners were known to visit Ash in the 19th century; whether they visited that particular farm is not known.

Maylam (1909, pp.79-94) devotes a significant section of his book wondering if the 'hood' of hoodening was connected to the 'hood' of Robin Hood, in particular the festive May or Robin Hood games. Robin and associated characters – a man/woman Maid Marian and a hobby horse – were particularly popular in pageantry during the Tudor period. The same hoodeners who visited Ash were reported to have a Maid Marian man/woman character along with fools and bladder sticks; although it is unclear whether the party named themselves that way, or if that was an interpretation of a Mr Solley, who reported it. As it is the only known instance of this association it is hard to draw any conclusions from it. Although the hobby horse was a common companion of the May festivities and dances, there is no evidence of it in the Robin Hood plays (Wiles 1981). In the earlier medieval ballad tradition (from the 1450-1550s) disguise is an important and repeated device (Holt 1989, p. 32). In one instance at least we come close to the notion of animal guising in the Middle English ballad Robin Hood and Guy of Gisborne. When Robin encounters him in the wood, Guy wears a "capull-hyde" or horse hide. "Topp, and tayle, and mayne", which sounds like a fairly complete costume. After killing him, Robin mutilates Guy's face so he can't be identified and switches clothes with him:

> Robin did his gowne of greene,
> On Sir Guye it throwe;
> And hee put on that capull-hyde,
> That cladd him topp to toe.
> (Knight and Ohlgren 1997)

The horse-hide disguise 'top to toe' is complete enough to trick the sheriff into thinking Guy has returned. I'm certainly not suggesting Guy's horse costume is anything like a hooden or hobby horse – it seems intended as a real horse's hide – but this is one rare and overlooked instance of a horse disguise in a medieval text. I mention this because if there was anything in it, Maylam's Robin Hood theory would so very neatly tie up the various sections of this exhibition: **The Kentish Hoodening Tradition**, **Hobby Horses and Obby Osses** and **Stag Guising**. But as Maylam was aware, the threads, though intriguing, are just not substantial enough to confirm a solid connection.

There are other things of note in Pegge's definition in his *Alphabet of Kenticisms*: he sees an analogy between hoodening, guising in Derbyshire, and the more widespread practice of mumming.

Today 'mumming' is a term usually applied to the 'hero-combat' type of 'folk drama', where a heroic character, often Saint or King George, combats a Turkish Knight or similar adversary. One or other is slain and then revived by a Doctor, who sometimes has some form of mock horse. Like so many 'folk' customs the hero-combat mummer's play was assumed to be ancient, but there are no traces of it before the 1730s. Such plays were especially popular around 1780-1900, and were spread by chapbooks. Some stock characters in the plays do have Tudor and Stuart antecedents (Traditional Drama Research Group 2017; Hutton 1994). Joseph Strutt's monumental *The Sports and Pastimes of the People of England* (1801) recognized the term mumming or 'mummeries' in much broader terms: "*Mumm* is said to be derived from the Danish word *mumme*, or *momme* in Dutch, and signifies to disguise oneself with a mask" (p.201). This is certainly consistent with its use in late Middle English. In the 15th and 16th centuries, festive costumes were generally referred to as mumming, masking or guising.

It is no accident that Pegge also mentions 'guising' in Derbyshire, as it was his native county. He makes many comparisons to Derbyshire customs throughout his dictionary of Kentish dialect. It was a good comparison to make, as Derbyshire guising involves mast-style animal disguises not unlike the hooden horse. We'll explore these traditions in the section on **The Northern Beasts**. The Middle

English word *guise* was used in the sense of one's outward appearance, costuming, masking or disguise; *guisers* being another word for mummers or maskers.

Although Pegge's definition hasn't mentioned a hooden horse, or any other character, he has indicated that it is a rural practice of masking at Christmas. So here his definition is consistent with the reports of hoodening performances that appear from 1807 onwards.

The earliest known description of a hoodening performance is at Ramsgate, in an anonymous letter to the editor of *European Magazine and London Review*, May 1807 (cited above by Doel). It states that "a party of young people procure the head of a dead horse" (Anon. 1807, p.358). Was the hooden horse once a skull head like those in the north of England and Wales? Or is the writer confusing it with those customs? It is an isolated statement; however towards the end of the century Charles Saunders of St Lawrence, Thanet wrote in a letter to *The Bromley Record* in 1889:

> A natural horse's head was rarely hired owing to the difficulty procuring one, but one carved from wood block was generally used as substitute. (Maylam 1909, p.36)

Mark Lawson (2018) of the Whitstable Hoodeners, a former zoo keeper and student of Biological Sciences, has suggested that as well as being quite heavy, a real horse's skull would shatter easily when dropped. Though a smaller colt skull might be lighter, it would be more brittle as the younger horse's bones would not be fully formed. Wood is altogether more robust and can be much lighter. So the notion of changing from a skull to wooden head is logical.

Who were the hoodeners?

Reports of hoodening from this period, the 19th century up until World War One, are concentrated in the north-eastern corner of East Kent, particularly around the Isle of Thanet, the villages surrounding Canterbury and the environs of Deal and Walmer. Other than isolated cases in Sittingbourne, Evington and Elham, the custom was exclusive to the farmed areas around the coast, the river Stour and around the old Wantsum Channel. Cawte (1978, pp.90-93) noted how distribution seemed to be connected with a certain type of soil and trade mobility using water, rather the migration patterns of the Saxons (to which some Victorian antiquarians like to attribute the custom). The area of the hooden horse is connected to specific agricultural practices where you would expect a heavy use of horsepower. The horse would have been especially meaningful as the primary mode of transportation as well as labour.

The social historian Malcolmson notes that in England, in the first half of the 18th century, around three quarters of people lived in villages, hamlets, scattered farmsteads and cottages. They made the bulk of their living directly from some form of agricultural work (1981, p.22-4). Wage labourers on farms had fairly consistent work from March to November but this fell off sharply in the winter months, when the weather restricted outdoor tasks and fuel needed purchasing (p.78). The subsistence of farm workers was highly precarious: thus the need to seek more money from activities like mumming, hoodening and carol singing. An analogous precarity in the modern world provides the focus of Post Workers Theatre's reinvention of mumming and hoodening, as we'll discuss in the section **What is Autohoodening?**

The hoodeners before the First World War were from working class trades. They were often farming labourers and stable hands; this was particularly noted at St Nicholas-at-Wade, Acol, Worth and Upper Walmer. But other trades were noted amongst performers, such as the boat trades in coastal Deal. The audience however were of all classes, depending on where the team chose to call during its perambulation. Teams visited town and village streets, pubs, shops and other workplaces as well as the houses of the wealthy, of landowners and middle class professionals.

The roles of working men as labourers, carters, shepherds and horsemen in the rural economy was different from that of women, meaning they had separate cultures of work. Folklorists in the 20th century often referred to mumming as the 'Men's Ceremonial' as if talking about a tribal secret initiation society, but there were more pragmatic reasons why folk drama was a male activity. The hoodeners and similar 'folk' customs seem to be exclusively male because they emerged from men's particular trades and their close working relationship with animals. This was the case at least before changes in working lives and the growth of cities in the early 20th century.

In a rural society where transportation was limited, working abroad might only be in the next parish. In the case of the hoodener George Goodson (originally from Preston near Wingham), we see how a folk performance might be spread from one area to another. At some point after 1902 he took his hooden horse and two labourers with him when he moved his service from Cleve Court Farm, Acol, to a farm at Felderland near Sandwich about 8 miles away (Maylam 1909, pp.48-49; Frampton 2018, p.58). In moving his labouring team he also moved his hoodening circuit, bringing any peculiarities of Thanet hoodening to the Sandwich area.

> In a society that lacks the means of rapid transport and communications, local peculiarities are likely to be highly developed, and people's sense of identity will be powerfully affected by the distinctive traditions and circumstances of their local environment. (Malcolmson 1981, p.93)

So, the localization of a culture within a defined agricultural area, like East Kent, is perhaps not surprising. What is surprising are the similarities in customs on a national level. This social situation fosters folk culture as something different from the culture of the educated middle and upper classes, who were writing history. Who are these 'folk' referred to in folk customs? As Bauman (1992, p. 34) said they are a people "grounded in shared identity". Malcolmson notes:

> Popular culture was…substantially independent of the culture of polite society. The people had their own traditions, their own beliefs, their own modes of expression. (1981, p.106)

With such a wide gulf between the classes it is no surprise that hoodening, mumming, and the like, escaped the attention of the literati before the 19th century. A sharp class division and sense of inequality was explicitly spelled out in Plough Plays in Nottinghamshire and Lincolnshire:

> We are not the London Actors
> That act upon the stage
> We are the country plough lads
> That ploughs for little wage.
> (cited in Tiddy 1923, pp.244-5; Chambers 1933, p.103)

Folk plays and hoodening were working class customs. Sometimes the local middle class and gentry viewed them with scorn, especially where excessive drinking and horseplay took place, and argued for their suppression. Others welcomed such players as a link to an increasingly romanticized rural past and encouraged them by regularly allowing them to perform at their homes and by giving money, food and drink. When a custom lapsed in a particular area, it was sometimes one of the local gentry who was instrumental in getting it revived (Cass and Roud 2002, p.40). However, after the First World War, as rural working life declined and new technology-driven popular entertainments appeared, both the audiences and performers of folk drama changed. The performers shifted from working men to middle class enthusiasts of both sexes. We will consider this changed social dynamic in the section **Reviving the Hooden Horse**.

What did they perform?

There are no surviving hoodening playscripts, or even mention of scripts, from the period before the First World War. But hoodeners did perform, often in a noisy, boisterous, improvised way and sometimes with song, music and jokes. Unlike professional drama there is no authoritative text. Instead, a tradition is expressed in its individual and varied instances:

> Rigidity, fossilization and formality are the hallmarks of authority; flexibility, alteration, and spontaneity are the hallmarks of folkloric performance. (Tillis, 1999, p.63)

Although there were some exceptions and variations, the hoodening performance would usually involve:

- The HOODEN HORSE – led by the Wagoner. It would cause mischief and throw anyone who tried to ride it.
- The WAGONER – reflected a real vocation in the horse-driven rural working culture in Kent. He would lead the wagon team and acted as a kind of overseer of farm hands.
- The JOCKEY/RIDER – attempted to ride the horse but would fall off. There were occasional reports of audience members participating by jumping on the back of the horse and trying to stay on.
- MOLLY – a man or boy dressed as a woman who tended to sweep before or after the horse with a besom broom. Characters of this type appear in many mumming plays throughout the country, sometimes called Bessie, Bet, Marian etc.
- MUSICIAN/s or SINGER/s – may have played parts above. Sometimes the team was accompanied by handbell ringers, a formerly popular entertainment throughout England since the Middle Ages.

In reports of some hoodening traditions of the 19th century (such as at St Nicholas-at-Wade and Walmer, documented by Maylam, 1909) performers blackened their faces. In mumming, guising and morris dancing traditions face-blackening is common but there is nothing to signify an intention of racial caricature, such as that seen in the exaggerations of the black-faced minstrels. The distinction between these different kinds of performers was drawn by Maylam who encountered a group of black-faced minstrels when searching the town for the Walmer Hoodeners (p.7). These minstrels were clearly an altogether different kind of act, profiting from racial stereotyping as entertainment.

Tillis (1999, p.188) noted the blackening of faces as widespread amongst mumming troupes, along with other kinds of masking. In cases where the actors in hero-combat plays blackened their faces, one might expect the Turkish Knight character to be blacked-up as a racial signifier, but instead it was a unified 'look' across all characters. Like a uniform costume, the blackening helps to hide the performers' individual identities. Blackening was reported in some of the earliest accounts of mumming plays:

> The mummeries practised by the lower classes of the people usually took place at the Christmas holidays; and such persons as could not procure masks rubbed their faces over with soot, or painted them… (Strutt 1801, p.202)

Strutt is clear that the blackening was a replacement for other kinds of fabricated mask. Using burnt cork or coal dust was the cheapest form of masking, and was used for this purpose rather than as racial mockery. But in Strutt we also find a disapproving tone about the way some mummers would behave when masked:

> It appears that many abuses were committed under the sanction of these disguisements; and for this reason an ordinance was established, by which a man was liable to punishment who appeared in the streets of London with a painted visage. (p.202)

This type of masking amongst some hoodening teams would have given the whole troupe license to misbehave, just as animal guising does.

Rather than being a survival of some distant and pure model as 19th century antiquarians supposed, the traditional performance is changeable from performance to performance, and performer to performer, but is related in content or form to a family of performances.

Tillis (1999, p.171) uses the biological terms homology and analogy to help explain the similarities between different forms of folk drama. Homologies are based on transmission from a common ancestor. Analogies are similarities formed by the pressures of similar environments. We can think about how much the similarities across the traditions have to do with the transmission from one region to another, perhaps through work, mobility and travel. And we can think about how similar the life of the farm labourer in Cheshire is to the experience of the equivalent worker in Kent.

For example, the plough plays in Lincolnshire and Nottinghamshire might be considered analogous to hoodening. They include characters such as Farmers Boy or Plough Boy and often refer to a horse, such as the play at Bulby, Lincolnshire:

> In comes I the Farmer's Boy
> Don't you see my whip in hand?
> Straight I go from end to end,
> Scarcely make a baulk or bend,
> To my horses I attend
> As they go marching round the end,
> Gee woa!
> (Tiddy 1923, p. 237)

Tiddy, who collected this play, doesn't indicate whether a horse disguise was used, but at least some kind of acting 'as-if' is indicated by the "Gee woa!". Clearly the plays are referring to the working horses pulling the plough. Chambers noted the inclusion of 'hobby horses' pulling ploughs at Somerby (1933, p.100). This similarity was close enough to confuse Cass and Roud (2002, p.103) who erroneously labelled the photograph of the St Nicholas Hoodeners c.1919 (**6**), as 'Derbyshire Plough Play'. A horse disguise given to Paula Jardine-Rose of the Wychling Hoodeners in 2002 at first sight appeared to be an old hooden horse bearing a sackcloth printed 'Wm. J. Gardner Ltd., Birchington Thanet', an agricultural merchant active from 1908 to 1956. However, it was rumoured that the former owner of the horse, George Henry Hope had constructed it in Lincolnshire in the 1980s using a sack that had been used to transport goods from Kent (Frampton 2018, p.204). So this horse could have originated either in Lincolnshire or in Kent and may have been used both in the plough play and hoodening traditions. It is difficult to draw conclusions about connections between the plough plays and hoodening but we can certainly point to the analogous experiences of farm boys and working horses in these different but similar contexts. Even the act of the horse throwing the rider is present in plough traditions, as it was presumably a regular accident in real life. For example at Goathland near Doncaster, South Yorkshire, a plough was taken around with a fisherman riding a 'hobby-donkey', and a character dies after being thrown from the horse (Chambers 1933, pp.124, 131).

Although some, or even most, of the examples in this catalogue might be considered analogies of hoodening there is a tradition in Dorset which is so close to hoodening in appearance, characters and action that it is difficult not to consider it homologous in some way. The mummers of Symondsbury (and formerly other nearby villages) perform a play which is consistent with hero-combat plays featuring St George elsewhere in the country. However, when the usual mock slaughter and resurrections have taken place a secondary drama (often referred to by antiquarians as a *quete*) begins, entirely independent of the hero-combat play.

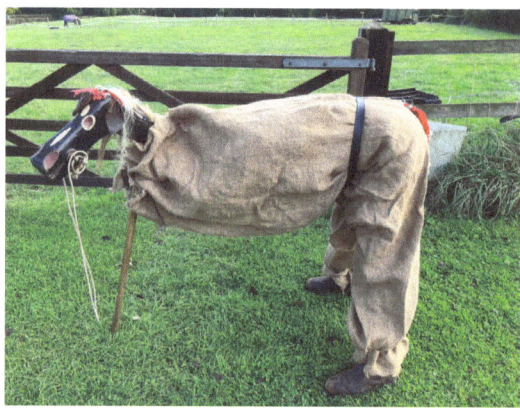

2 Symondsbury Mummers' 'Tommy' hobby horse, Dorset (pre-20th century)

Credit: Harry Harrison (St George!), Symondsbury Mummers

In the filmed documentation of the Symondsbury play (*Walk in St. George* 1952) the second section is titled 'The Hobby Horse'. What enters is a very similar construction to a hooden horse but with an extended carved neck (**2**). 'Tommy' is carved and painted much like the St Nicholas-at Wade hooden horse. The performer is hooded under a hessian sackcloth and also wears hessian trousers.

In the play the man dressed as a woman called Old Bet, much like the hooders' Molly, enters astride 'Tommy' the horse. With them is a male character called Jan, who plays the part of the would-be jockey. He wears a labourer's smock and a top hat, appearing much like the Wagoner in hoodening. After mocking the poor state of the horse, Jan attempts to ride the him but is thrown (like the hoodening Jockey). Jan then beats the horse and kills it:

> BET   You naughty old rogue. You have killed my pony, you have, you old rogue.
> JAN   What did'st bring that kicking thing in here for? To kick a man's brains out? Tell 'ee what we'll do, Bet – we'll have a leaf-twiddick and bouse him up.
> BET   Bouse you up, you old rogue.
> JAN   Throw down your stick, blow in your hands, and beat, beat lusty, beat till your eyes do sparkle, now kneel down (holds hands over pony). Be ready?
> BET   Yes.
> JAN   Now then, up.
> *(They swing their hands after the manner of labourers on a cold day and hold their hands over the pony as though to convey warmth to him.)*
> *(Bet falls down)*

Together, Jan and Bet revive the horse who then performs mock fortune-telling as a form of audience participation:

> BET   My pony tells fortunes, Jan.
> JAN   Tell fortunes do her? Well, what will her tell?
> BET   Now Tommy you go round and tell me the little boy that pinches his mother's sugar.
> *(Tommy finds the boy in the crowd of spectators)*
> BET   Is that the one? Now Tommy you go round and find out the little girl who throws the bed clothes off in the morning whilst dreaming about her sweetheart?
> *(Tommy finds her out by nodding in front of her)*
> BET   Now Tommy you go round and find out the biggest rogue that's in here and throw him right through the door.
> *(Tommy kicks Jan out)*
> (Kennedy 1952, pp.9–11)

The Symondsbury mummers were active from at least 1870 until 1900 and then revived after the victory celebrations in 1945, shortly before they were filmed. The horse's head had been recovered from a loft above a stable in the 1930s or 1940s. It has since been furnished with a new pole and hessian and is used by the current Symondsbury team. A similar play in nearby Evershot was recorded by the BBC in 1936, its costumes dated to the 19th century. Here, Father Christmas knocked down the horse and attempted to ride him at the end (Cawte 1978, pp.148-152).

Kennedy (1952) recognized the close connection with Kentish hoodening. It is so tempting to wonder whether this text represents something like a lost hoodening play, wherever it originated or evolved. At the very least we might consider it like a missing link between the isolated hoodeners of East Kent and the fairly widespread mumming plays in the rest of the country, where a more frequent presence than the horse is the Molly-type character. Geoff Doel and Nick Miller noticed the very close family resemblance and integrated a Doctor, the horse's fortune telling device and other lines into their play with the Tonbridge Hoodeners from 1979 onwards (Appendix 2).

Why did they do it?

Writers on folk performance throughout the 19th century saw hoodening, other animal guising, and mumming, as having their origins in ancient agricultural fertility rites. In particular they looked to the ritual killing of ancient kings in James Frazer's *The Golden Bough* (1890). Although Frazer (1890a, pp.57-99) didn't mention folk drama or animal guising specifically, his presentation of the English Jack-in-the Green and May Pole dancing as echoes of a sacrificial vegetation god was hugely influential. However, his erroneous footnote (1890b, p.211) about morris dancers as a custom exclusively associated with Plough Monday shows how little he knew of its widespread distribution.

Following Frazer, folklorists would refer to mumming or guising in terms of 'ceremony' or 'ritual' rather than say, 'theatrical performance' (Chambers 1933; Cawte, Helm and Peacock 1967; Brody 1970). However, they were often aware of the gulf between what the performers thought they were doing and what the theorists said they were doing: "…it is not suggested for one moment that towards the close of the 19th century…the performers seriously considered or understood the primitive ritual they were continuing" (Cawte, Helm and Peacock 1967, p. 25).

This Frazerian position has been challenged more recently. Craig Fees (1994) reiterated how different in perspective the performer and antiquarian writer were. This he saw as a class barrier between the 'folk' who participated and the far-removed library-based scholars who studied them. Furthermore, the rural working class were not isolated from 'professional' drama, but often integrated elements of touring shows in their own entertainments:

Eighteenth and nineteenth century folk were living in a theatrical age. Professional actors, going up and down the professional ladder, performed at local fairs under conditions that can make the folk play look refined. (p.3)

What we call the mumming play fits quite neatly into the eclectic repertoire of touring companies in this period, but as a localized form. Harrop (2020, pp.8-9) extends this argument and demonstrates how the mumming plays transcribed and described in the 18th and 19th century were parodies of 17th century heroic dramas. They even overplayed the old-fashioned phrases to appear more antiquated, conveying a sense of history and nostalgia. We should therefore think about how much folk performers, with their hazy notion of origins, might have been playing to this middle-class desire for rural nostalgia.

For Bauman (1992), tradition is not static and unchanging; it is dialectical. It is a back-and-forth interaction between the communal tradition and individual innovations. Following him, Tillis (1999) talked about tradition not being immutable and canon, but varied and dynamic: a "superorganic entity" (pp.53-54). Tillis's definition of folk drama discards the previous generation's emphasis on ritual. For him 'folkloric drama' is:

- based on living tradition
- is not fixed by authority
- engenders or enhances a sense of community (pp.137-140)

Tillis's final point here, about a sense of community, provides an alternative explanation of folk drama. In this sense, hoodening was a localized entertainment expressing the particular social conditions of its performers. It helped to bind the community during the Christmas season and crossed class barriers between performers and audience. Though I can see the attraction of the ritual survival theory, one problem is the implication that the custom is effectively defunct; as if the performers are mechanically trotting out a dramatic structure that they no longer understand. Although a custom like hoodening may evidence a surviving echo of a past way of life, the strength of the Tillis's social theory of the folk play is that it recognizes how hoodening can continue to have a communal purpose.

Summary

Hoodening is a folkloric performance which developed amongst the working class in the eastern corner of Kent. There are many analogies to the customs and rural way of life found elsewhere in the country. However, a mumming tradition in Dorset seems to be very close to hoodening in appearance, characterization and spirit. There is no obvious sense that one thing has influenced or been derived from another; instead we might think about cross-fertilization and family resemblances between customs.

Hooden horses are performing objects with a past and a genealogy. They have a home and a region of influence; they also have a family resemblance to each other and to customs in different regions. The history and origins of hoodening and the hooden horse, like so many so-called folk customs, is sometimes lost, confused and often romanticized. The impossibility of tracing an origin of this or any other folk custom in any linear way might lead us towards other models of understanding culture. Instead of a chain of customs, each originating in something earlier, we should think of a complex network of influences. This way of thinking may help us comprehend both the differing localization and the similarities between animal guising practices across the country.

Bibliography

Alford, V. (1978) *The Hobby Horse and Other Animal Masks*. London: Merlin Press.

Anon. (1807) 'Curious Custom in the Isle of Thanet' in *European Magazine and London Review* 51, p.358.

Bauman, R. (1992) 'Folklore', in Bauman, R. (ed.) *Folklore, Cultural Performances, and Popular Entertainments: A Communications-centred Handbook*. Oxford University Press, pp.29–40.

Brody, A. (1969) *English Mummers and their Plays: Traces of Ancient Mystery*. London: Routledge and Kegan Paul.

Cass, E. and Roud, S. (2002) *Room, Room, Ladies and Gentleman: An Introduction to the English Mummer's Play*. London: English Folk Dance and Song Society and The Folklore Society.

Cawte, E.C. (1978) *Ritual Animal Disguise: A Historical and Geographical Study of Animal Disguise in the British Isles*. Cambridge: D.S. Brewer.

Cawte, E.C., Helm, A. and Peacock, N. (1967) *English Ritual Drama*. London: The Folk-lore Society.

Chambers, E.K. (1933) *The English Folk Play*. Oxford: Oxford University

Fees, C. (1994) 'Damn St. George! Some Neglected Home Truths in the History of British Folk Drama, or Bring Out Your Dead', in *Traditional Drama Studies* 3, pp.1–14.

Frampton, G. (2018) *Discordant Comicals: The Christmas Hooveners of East Kent, Tradition and Revival*. 2nd edn. St Nicholas-at-Wade: Ozaru Books

Frazer, James (1890a) *The Golden Bough: A Study in Comparative Religion Vol. I*. New York and London: Macmillan and Co, 1894.

Frazer, James (1890b) *The Golden Bough: A Study in Comparative Religion Vol. II*. New York and London: Macmillan and Co, 1894.

Harrop, P. (2020) *Mummer's Plays Revisited*. London: Routledge.

Holt, J.C. (1989) *Robin Hood*. 2nd edn. London: Thames and Hudson.

Hutton, R. (1996) *The Stations of the Sun: A History of the Ritual Year in Britain*. Oxford: Oxford University Press.

Hutton, R. (1994) *The Rise and Fall of Merry England*. Oxford: Oxford University Press.

Kennedy, P. (1952) 'The Symondsbury Mumming Play', in *Journal of the English Folk Dance and Song Society* 7 (1), 1952, pp.1–12.

Knight, S. and Ohlgren, T. (eds.) (1997) *Robin Hood and Other Outlaw Tales*. Kalamazoo, Michigan: Medieval Institute Publications. Available at: https://d.lib.rochester.edu/teams/publication/knight-and-ohlgren-robin-hood-and-other-outlaw-tales

Lawson, M. (2018) Interview with James Frost, 8 March.

Malcolmson, R.W. (1981) *Life and Labour in England 1700–1780*. London: Hutchinson & Co.

Maylam, P. (1909) *The Hooden Horse, An East Kent Christmas Custom*. Canterbury: Percy Maylam.

Maylam, R., Lynn, M. and Doel, G. (2009) *Percy Maylam's The Kent Hooden Horse*. Stroud: The History Press.

Pegge, S. (1735–6) 'Alphabet of Kenticisms, and Collection of Proverbial Sayings used in Kent' in *Archæologia Cantiana* 9, 1874, pp.50–147.

Skeat, W.W. (1882) *An Etymological Dictionary of the English Language*. Oxford: Clarendon Press.

Strutt, J. (1801) *Sports and Pastimes of the People of England*. London: Methuen & Co.

Tiddy, R.J.E. (1923) *The Mummer's Play*. Oxford: Oxford University

Tillis, S. (1999) *Rethinking Folk Drama*. Westport, Connecticut: Greenwood

Traditional Drama Research Group (2017) *Folk Play Research Website*, available at: https://folkplay.info

Walk in St George (1952) directed by Alan Simpson. UK: English Folk Dance and Song Society

Wiles, D. (1981) *The Early Plays of Robin Hood*. Cambridge: D.S. Brewer.

THE EXHIBITS

James Frost

The Kentish Hoodening Tradition

Image on preceding page:

3 'Dobbin' of the St Nicholas-at-Wade Hoodeners (June 1905)
Credit: Henry Beauchamp Collis

4 'Dobbin', St Nicholas-at-Wade hooden horse (pre-20th century)
St Nicholas-at-Wade with Sarre Hoodeners
Credit: James Frost

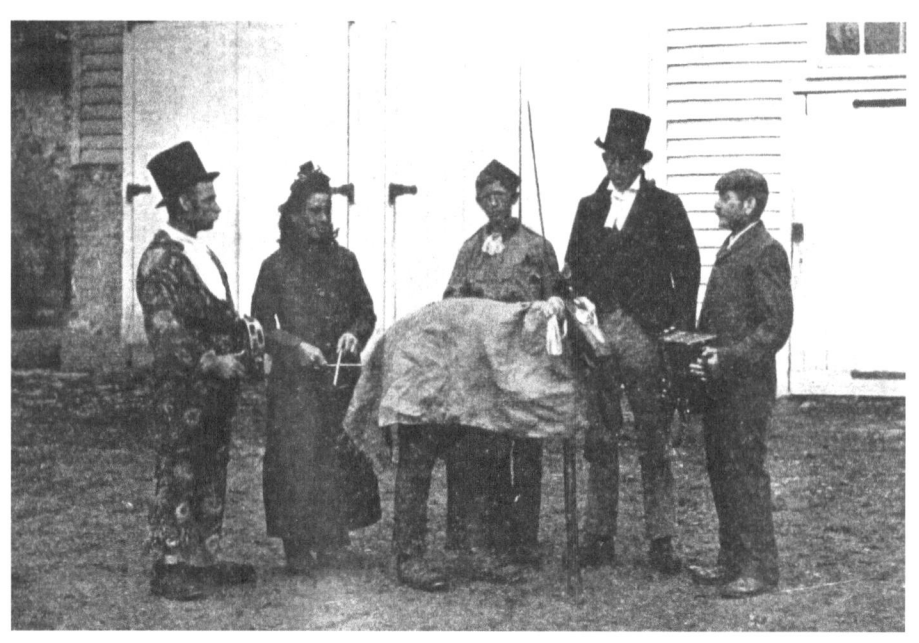

5 'Dobbin' with the St Nicholas-at-Wade Hoodeners (June 1905)
Credit: Henry Beauchamp Collis

'Dobbin' was named by the St Nicholas-at-Wade Hoodeners and is used today in their Christmas performances (**4**). This long-serving relic is a direct link with the old hoodening tradition, as it was first documented. Dobbin is connected to a past that we can see through old photographs, and read through reports of performances. In 1905 Dobbin was photographed with a much earlier hoodening team at Bolingbroke Farm in Sarre (**5**), a 45-minute walk from St Nicholas and part of their performance circuit. The photographer from Canterbury, Henry Beauchamp Collis, was employed by Percy Maylam (1909, p.5) for his book on the subject. Although the team would normally perform in winter, the light was considered unreliable, and so the photographs were taken in June.

Dobbin appears again in a photograph taken around 1919 (dated by Frampton 2018), after the interruption of the First World War, with a new, young team (**6**). In 1966 Tristan Jones reformed the St Nicholas team after coming across Dobbin in a display of rural bygones at the St Nicholas Primary School the previous year. Four of the Trice brothers who had been members of the team, photographed around 1919 and 1921, were still alive and Edmund Trice had Dobbin in his possession (Jones 2018). The young jockey standing behind Dobbin in the 1919 photo is Tom West. West and Mrs Trice were interviewed by Tristan Jones in 1977 (Frampton 2018, pp.62–68). Both said that the object of the performance was primarily to make money at Christmas, performing in pubs, shops and big houses.

They referred to the 'great walk' on one of those nights, which was around 16 kilometers (p.92).

6 'Dobbin' with the St Nicholas-at-Wade Hoodeners (c.1919)
Credit: English Folk Dance and Song Society

They did not perform a scripted play, but to all accounts they larked around, telling jokes and engaging in horseplay. At times the performances sounded quite raucous. West recalled the horse throwing him into a pile of biscuit tins at the bakery, and over the counter at the King's Head, but was keen to point out that "no furniture was damaged" on their visits. In a further interview with Martin Beale of the reformed team in 1983, West elaborated on the physical strain of the performance:

> (It was a rough affair) from my point of view. The others, they were all right. But I was the one who was getting all the buffeting about and sprawling around. The horse always used to be someone pretty hefty, and once he'd had two or three drinks…well, that was it. It was just unbearable. I went home with more knocks and bruises than was healthy, I think. (pp.68–70)

Rather than singing deeply meaningful and archaic folk songs, as one might expect, they used the popular music hall and variety song sheets available from Woolworths (although the song 'Farmers Boy' may have resonated with their backgrounds as farm workers). The Wagoner was a key character leading the hooden horse, and West's father was a wagoner by trade, working with real horses. Other than the hooden horse and the Jockey, the hoodeners blackened their faces with burnt cork as a disguise, although it is not clear if this is the case in the earliest photographs (see discussion above in the section **What was Hoodening?**).

Maylam (1909, pp.2–3) himself had seen the St Nicholas Hoodeners perform every Christmas in a Thanet farmhouse (Gore Street, Monkton) from 1888 to 1892. The performance was enacted by farm hands who wore smock frocks "years ago" and occasionally blackened their faces as disguise. The Wagoner entered cracking his whip, leading the 'Hoodener' (Horse). The Rider, followed by audience members, attempted to mount the horse who tried to unseat him. Molly, a lad dressed as a woman, swept behind the horse with a birch broom and was known to stand on his/her head revealing corduroy trousers and hobnail boots (cited above by Doel). There were no set words for performance and songs and carols were not usual. By comparing West's account with Maylam's observations we can see that the custom remained fairly consistent from one St Nicholas team to another.

The earliest known report of a St Nicholas hoodening team is perhaps the account of Rev. H. Bennett Smith, Vicar of St Nicholas-at-Wade in 1876:

> I made an enquiry of an old farmer in my parish, as to the custom called Hoodning [sic]. He tells me that formerly the farmer used to send annually round the neighbourhood the best horse under the charge of the wagoner, and that afterwards instead, a man used to represent the horse, being supplied with a tail, and with a wooden [pronounced ooden or hooden] figure if [sic] a horse's head, and plenty of horse hair for a mane. The horse's head was fitted with hobnails for teeth; the mouth being made to open by means of a string, and in closing made a loud crack. The custom has long since ceased. (Parish and Shaw 1888, p.77)

This report greatly annoyed Maylam (1909, p.23), who dismisses it as inaccurate and unreliable. For a start, the custom had not ceased, but this was a common statement in records of continuing customs around the country. The substitution of a real horse for a wooden one is an intriguing suggestion when we consider the plough traditions and numerous horse skull disguises elsewhere in the country.

In his father Tristan's notebooks, Ben Jones found the suggestion that the hooden horse Dobbin may have been made towards the end of the 19th century by Arthur Bolton of St Nicholas (Jones 2018). Dobbin has a long rectangular wooden head with minimal carving, eyes set staring upwards from the plank, and leather ears. He is decorated like a working horse on show at a fair with a decorative brass sun disk and triple-belled turret, a bridle, and ribbons in his mane (known as 'caytis'). This particular aesthetic, or family resemblance, can be seen in other early surviving horses and has influenced numerous later constructions. Dobbin's pole has been repaired with two iron sleeves, in a manner typical of farm implement repairs in the 19th century and earlier. If we compare photographs there is a slight discolouration at the bottom of the pole in 1905 (**3** & **5**), as if it is muddy or rotten. In photographs taken around 1919 and 1921 (**6** & **1**) we can see a distinct repair to the pole. Also, in 1905 Dobbin had a mirror turret, described by Maylam as a 'swinging disk' (1909, p. 16). In 1919 and 1921 this has been replaced by the triple-belled turret.

7 Chislet hooden horse (1906, repainted 2009)
Miles Collection, Rosamund Horne (née Miles) custodian
Credit: Hazel Tasker

A hooden horse remarkably similar to Dobbin was discovered in 1972 by Chris Smith, former landlord of the Gate Inn at Marshside near Chislet (**7**). After witnessing a performance by the reformed St Nicholas Hoodeners, Smith realized he had a hooden horse hanging in the roof of his recently purchased barn in the village of Millbank near Hoath (a few miles away), which he had assumed to be a child's hobby horse. The barn was previously occupied by the Miles family. Ethel Miles confirmed it had been made by her grandfather Bert (Herbert Henry Miles), a carpenter, around 1906 when she was a small child. She witnessed its construction but still found it terrifying (Small 1976; Frampton 2018, p.74–6). Bert Miles had arranged for the St Nicholas team to be photographed by Collis for Maylam's book in 1905 (1909, p.5). So he made this horse in the style of Dobbin very shortly after those photographs, obviously inspired by the new interest in hoodening.

Smith hung the horse behind his bar for a number of years before it was returned to the descendants of the Miles family. When found it had a battered head and pole, and was missing its cloth, but has since been repaired and repainted.

8 Hooden horse found at Wingham (c.1900–1910)
Maidstone Museum
Credit: James Frost

The larger of the hooden horses held at Maidstone Museum closely resembles both the St Nicholas Dobbin and Chislet horse with its rectangular head, leather ears and flat carved eyes (**8**). It was found, along with a smaller hooden horse (like a young colt) (**10**), in a barn in Wingham, by students of the Wye Agricultural College. It was presented to the Museum in 1956 (Grove 1956, p.273). According to Barnett Field (1967, p.204) another head of a hooden horse was found around the same time at Guston, but what happened to it is not known (see discussion of **17**, below).

The two horses at Maidstone Museum may have come from a team, mentioned by Maylam (1909, p.50), which visited Stourmouth and Preston-next-Wingham. In a letter to Tristan Jones the former curator of Maidstone Museum, Graham Hunter, stated that "the more elaborate dates from 1900–1910" and the "plain one" from around 30 years earlier (Frampton 2018, p.88). Presumably Hunter was referring to the Dobbin-like horse as 'elaborate' because of its brasses and caytis, and the smaller colt as 'plain'. The 'elaborate' Wingham horse has a lightweight cotton covering, now much decayed. It is sun-bleached but was originally of a dark, thin material. Underneath the horse's head is a deteriorated black stocking. Most likely this would have contained cushioning for the performer's head, when crouched ready for the rider to jump on. Its teeth appear to be small pebbles rather than hobnails. Like its cousins, it is decorated with red rosettes, a studded rein, and sun disk horse brass. Its decorative mirror turret affixed to the rear of its head is much like the one seen on Dobbin in 1905, and we might wonder whether it is in fact the same turret. Amy Bracey (2017) of the Maidstone Carriage Museum explains:

> The piece of metalwork in the pictures is a decorative turret from heavy horse harness. When the horses were decorated for show and pageants the saddle pads, collars and bridles would be covered with gleaming brass ornamentation. Because these swing they would catch the light and add to the dazzling spectacle. I think they were in use from the late 19th century.

9 'Wingham' hooden horse (c.1910-1939)
Maylam Family Archives
Credit: Gordon Chase

In a pair of photographs still in the possession of the Maylam family, a hooden horse is seen alongside an unidentified man in a farm labourer's smock (**Cover & 9**). Close examination of these photographs reveals that this is indeed the 'Wingham' horse of Maidstone Museum. Notice, in the close-up, how the studded rein, sun disk, mirror turret, dark but lightweight fabric, caytis, triangular ears and the position of its teeth precisely match the 'Wingham' horse. The only visible difference is that the rosette has been changed. The photograph frame is embossed 'Gordon Chase, Bromley and Beckenham' where his photographic studios were registered from 1913 (Bond 2022). In his foreword of Dec 1909, Maylam was clear that the only extant horses he knew about were those he reproduced from Collis's photographs. This is consistent with Maylam either commissioning or acquiring Chase's photograph from 1913 onwards. There is no indication of where this photograph was taken or to which hoodening team it belonged at the time.

10 'Colt' hooden horse found at Wingham (c.1870–1880)
Maidstone Museum
Credit: James Frost

11 'Walmer Court' hooden horse (c.1850s)
Deal Museum
Credit: James Frost

Maidstone Museum's small 'Colt' (**10**) was dated by Hunter as the earlier of the two 'Wingham' hooden horses. Its wooden head is more rounded than its companion and coloured in the distinctive red, white and black scheme as the other horses we have looked at from Thanet and the Stourmouth marshes. It is wearing a very smart horse jacket which is clearly not original as there are traces of earlier sackcloth visible underneath. Also, there is evidence of leather fixings which have been cut and traces of real horse hair mane. Like Dobbin, it has metal stud teeth and leather ears. It is decorated with rosettes but doesn't appear to have had a decorative turret. The mouth string comes through the top of the head, and has worn the wood down from repeated pulling. This horse has had a lot of wear and tear, but has also been renewed at some point.

Whether either or both of these horses were used by an old Wingham hoodening team, or if they just ended up being stored in the parish, is impossible to say. If they were used by the same team, it is tempting to imagine the smaller colt being used by younger team members before progressing to the heavier and more decorative beast.

12 'Walmer Court' Hoodeners (1907)
Credit: Henry Beauchamp Collis

An adult (**11**) and companion colt hooden horse (**13**) also features in the Deal Museum collection. The traditions at the coastal town of Deal and rural Upper Walmer were well documented by Maylam and both teams were photographed by Collis in 1909 and 1907.

13 Walmer 'Colt' hooden horse (1955)
Deal Museum
Credit: James Frost

The horse of the Walmer Court Farm Hoodeners has miraculously survived and is well preserved with intact caytis and rosettes. Maylam (1909, pp.7–9) had observed the custom at Upper Walmer going back to at least 1849. The men of Walmer Court Farm would take the horse out around the town, led by one man and accompanied by a couple of musicians, but not with the characters familiar elsewhere. Formerly, they wore farm labourers' smocks, like the St Nicholas Hoodeners.

In 1955 the horse was rediscovered by Barnett Field, a champion of local customs, at Coldblow Farm in Walmer where it had been stored since 1912. On the same day Field wandered Walmer until he found one of the old hoodeners, Joseph 'Jack' Lamming (then aged 82), who appears in Collis's photograph as a young man holding a tambourine (Field 1967, p.204). Jack's uncle had operated the horse, his father played the accordion and his brother the triangle (**12**). According to one report his grandfather, an actual wagoner, had made the old horse (Frampton 2018, p.106). Notice what a long, almost crocodilian mouth this horse has. Like the St Nicholas Dobbin, it has rosettes and a three-bell turret, but one mounted on the top rather than the back of its head. Unlike the photographs of other old hooden horses this example is standing upright, as Maylam (1909, p. 9) said it was "fond of rearing".

14 Robert John Thomas Skardon and the Deal hooden horse (1909)
Credit: Henry Beauchamp Collis

Old Jack Lamming was so taken with Field's interest and attempts to revive the custom that he made this colt from driftwood shortly before his death in 1956 (**13**). Field donated both horses to Folkestone Library, Museum and Art Gallery and they were moved to Deal Maritime and Local History Museum in 1999. The colt imitates the construction and mechanism of Walmer Court horse but with a shorter nose, and the addition of a hole at the back of the throat, with sock attached inside, for collecting money. Both horses have matching turquoise bands, likely to have been added by either Lamming or Field.

15 Instruments of the North Deal Band and horse whip
Deal Museum
Credit: James Frost

The Deal Hoodeners' horse which appears in Collis's photo from 1909 (**14**) was apparently still functional in 1953 but was soon after, sadly "got rid of" (Frampton 2018, p.104). Bob Skardon, a fishmonger by trade, appears in the photograph playing a concertina to the horse, whose cloth was actually of dark green. He had known the custom since the 1850s and had carried the horse as a lad. Like the Walmer Court Horse, the Deal horse only went out with musicians, though apparently there had once been a Molly-like character called Daisy (Maylam 1909, pp.45–47). Music seemed to be a central part of their team and the members overlapped with the North Deal Band who played nautical songs for functions, apparently disbanding before the First World War. The members of the group had other trades related to boats, including an 'iggler' (who dealt goods from wrecked vessels) as their fiddler. A number of their instruments and a horse whip have survived and are kept in the Deal Museum (**15**).

16 Julia Small's 'Hengist' (c.1970s)
Deal Museum
Credit: James Frost

The Deal Hoodeners and North Deal Band mostly worked in trades connected to ship maintenance, the economy of Deal being largely maritime. So the importance of the horse may have had a slightly different resonance to that of the farm-based hoodeners elsewhere. We might wonder whether they were aware of the fairly widespread horse burial ceremony at sea, or its accompanying shanty. Sailors joining a ship were allowed a month's pay in advance: a metaphorical 'dead horse'. After a month at sea, a dead horse effigy was given a sea burial. The horse effigy was built around a barrel, and pushed around deck with a sailor playing the part of jockey. The whole crew processed singing the 'Burial of the Dead Horse' sea shanty. The horse was sold by auction to any passengers (presumably as a fundraiser for the sailors) but rather than receive the horse, it was hauled to yard arm with the jockey astride it. The jockey dismounted, cut the rope, and the horse plummeted overboard. The shanty emphasizes the fate of real horses, too old for working use and fated to be slaughtered and salted for sailors' meat (Tangye 1883, pp.21–23; Richards 1897, pp.281–4; Hugill 1969, pp.98–99).

A short-lived revival of hoodening took place in Deal in the late 1970s with a driftwood horse named 'Hengist' made by Julia Small, former secretary of Deal, Walmer and District Local History Society and volunteer at Deal Museum (**16**). Small has recently donated Hengist, who does not appear in this exhibition, for display there.

17 Deal Hoodeners' Horse (1997)
Deal Hoodeners
Credit: Deal Hoodeners

A further revival in 1997, led by Gill and Chris Nixon, included a Molly, musicians and a new horse with green fabric covering (**17**), based on the original Deal horse (**14**). Following the guidance of Jim Skardon, grandson of Bob Skardon (in Collis's photograph), their focus was on Christmas carolling and nautical songs (Frampton 2018, p.135–8). At the time of writing, this Deal hoodening team are still active.

18 'Satan' hooden horse (pre-20th century)
St Nicholas-at-Wade with Sarre Hoodeners
Credit: James Frost

Not all discoveries are as easy to identify as the Walmer Court horse or St Nicholas Dobbin. In 1976 Tristan Jones, who had revived the St Nicholas Hoodeners, found a fascinating wooden horse head on a short pole in a Canterbury antique shop (**18**). It was bizarrely labelled '18th century Italian hat-snatcher' but the dealer agreed it was English and it had been acquired near Tunbridge Wells a couple of years previously, supporting the notion of it being a Kentish hooden horse (Frampton 2018, p.203, Jones 2018). Its head is carved from a heavy hard wood, possibly oak. It is more like a real horse's head in shape than any other surviving hooden horse. Like the St Nicholas Dobbin, Chislet and Wingham horses, it is painted black with white band on bridge of nose and red nostrils. Its bottom jaw is fixed to a (longer, replacement) pole and the top jaw moves. Rather than individual teeth it has cast metal plates inside the mouth which are most likely to be heel plates, commonly attached to the bottom of workers' and military hobnail boots. Its ears move forward and backwards on a lever system. It is decorated with a bell turret attached to the forehead. It has a bridle with a rosette and a braid attached to the harness. Like many other hooden horses its covering is of hessian.

Examining the inner cavity of its head it is clear that the eyes were once bored holes. They have since been filled in and painted as protrusions. Metal fixings inside the inner top hollow of the head, near the eyes, suggest that there was once a cradle there for holding a small candle, possibly two, or a very small oil lantern. This detail was noted in a horse that was seen at Hoath in the 1880s (some time before the making of the one found by Chris Smith in the same parish). The horse described had "two holes bored through the forehead to form the eyes" to see the glow of the candle (cited above by Doel, and Maylam 1909, p.28). Furthermore, the top of the hollow of Satan's head is covered in what appears to be very old soot deposits. There are traces of red paint around the inside of the hollow, which would have made the mouth glow red with reflected light from the candles.

The insertion of a light within the horse's head is not feasible in the Dobbin-type of horse; the head needs to be taller and hollowed, like Satan's, to comfortably accommodate it. But where is Satan from? Is it the horse seen in Hoath in the 1880s? The same report suggests there was more than one hooden horse in the parish. Is Satan the horse found at Guston around 1950, which then vanished?

Aaron Janes suggested Satan might be the original Lower Hardres 'Christmas Horse', described as being "more like a horse" with a white streak on its forehead and a distinct neck (Maylam 1909, pp.53–55). Although Satan does not have such a neck, it could reasonably describe the way the horse was performed, with the pole being pushed upwards to extend the neck. A Lower Hardres team was active before 1857, visiting the villages to the south and south west of Canterbury, until they disbanded around 1892. The Lower Hardres horse collected coins between its jaws, which is feasible for Satan. It had glossy black material instead of sacking, but this could easily have been replaced. The legend recounted by Maylam was that in Christmas 1859, a German woman leapt out of her wheelchair with fright upon seeing the horse, and was thereafter miraculously able to walk again. Her husband bought the horse at the end of the season; thus the Lower Hardres team was required to replace their horse. Alternatively, the Lower Hardres horse may have been more like the Symondsbury Tommy, with its visible neck and white streak on the forehead (**2**).

Tristan Jones's St Nicholas hoodening team named this horse 'Satan' because they considered it scarier and more mischievous than their other horses, especially at night. Unless some very old photographs turn up, there is no way of confirming its origin.

Image on preceding page:

19 The 'Brown Horse' at Folkestone International Folk Festival (1985)
Credit: Folkestone International Folklore Festival Archive courtesy of Folkestone Town Council

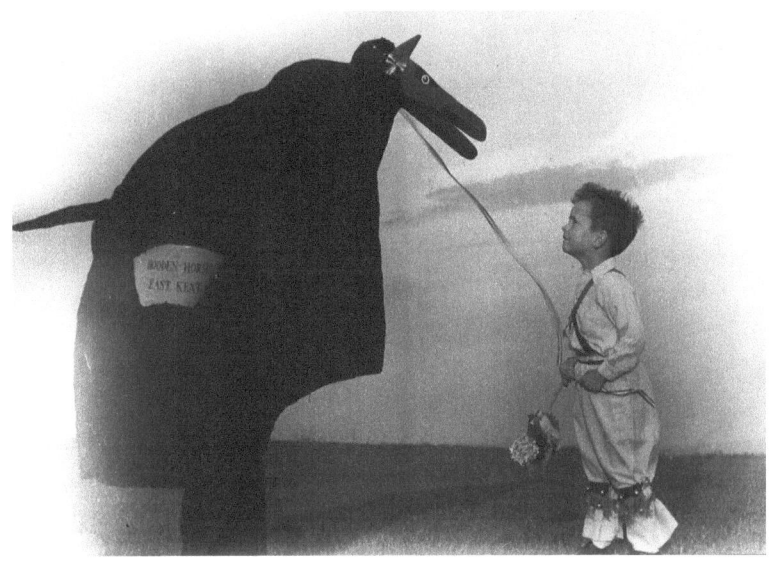

20 The 'Brown Horse' and John Field in morris dancing kit at the Queen's Coronation celebrations (1953)
Credit: English Folk Dance and Song Society

21 Barnett Field and the 'Brown Horse'
Credit: Folkestone International Folklore Festival Archive courtesy of Folkestone Town Council

22 Barnett and Olive Field's 'Brown Horse' (1953)
John Field Collection
Credit: James Frost

Perhaps the most travelled, and certainly the most photographed, of the revival hooden horses was the 'Brown Horse' made by Olive and Barnett Field for the Folkestone Coronation celebrations in 1953 (**19–22, 24**). According to Barnett Field it was based loosely on Collis's photograph of the destroyed Deal horse (**14**, Field 1967, p.204). Of note are its decorative horse brasses – the top one is commemorative of the Queen's Coronation, while below it is one gifted by a Dutch dancing team at the first Folkestone International Folklore Festival. On the side of its head the Brown Horse sports badges of the East Kent Morris Men representing Invicta, the white horse symbol of Kent, along with patriotic red, white and blue rosette and ribbons. A copy of this hooden horse is still used by Rabble Folk Theatre led by Gail Duff.

23 The Beckenham Morris Dancers with a hooden horse, fed by a fool (1950)

Credit: English Folk Dance and Song Society

The Fields were important figures in the national and international promotion of English folk traditions from the 1950s until the 1980s. Barnett Field, a retired bank manager, and Olive, a P.E. teacher, were folk enthusiasts who were inspired after seeing the Ravensbourne Morris Dancers of Bromley at the Chilham Castle Festival. Ravensbourne were perfoming with a hooden horse that had been passed on from Beckenham Morris after the war (**23**). Beckenham were apparently the first morris side to perform with a hooden horse on 15 July 1939 at the Kent District Folk Dance Festival (Frampton 2018, p.114). Thus the habitat of the hooden horse expanded. Hooden horses were evolving from being an exclusive feature of the East Kent Christmas to being widely seen at folk festivals and events with morris sides around the country.

24 Olive Field (centre) with the Handbell Hoodeners and 'Brown Horse', at Folkestone International Folklore Festival
Credit: Folkestone International Folklore Festival Archive courtesy of Folkestone Town Council

The Fields' original Brown Horse regularly appeared around the UK and abroad, with the groups they had founded: the East Kent Morris Men and the Handbell Hoodeners (**24**). In a report from The Castle pub near Hythe, the East Kent Morris Men's performance involved the horse dying and the Fool calling out for a 'District Nurse'. A "pretty but rather bewildered girl" was picked from the audience to revive the horse with a kiss (Field and Field 1983, p.37). When the horse stood up all the dancers laid down to die, which must have been highly comical.

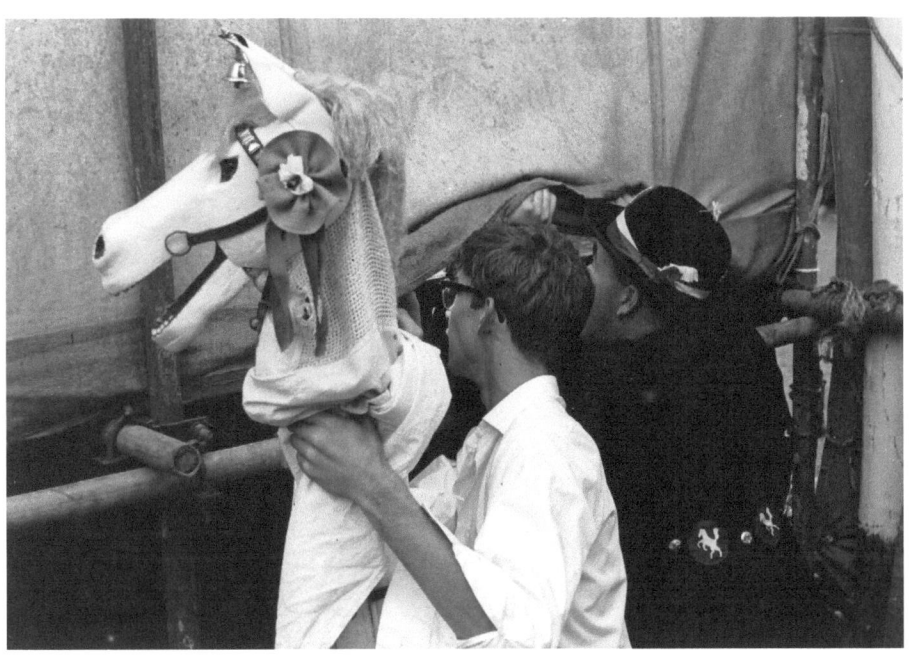

25 East Kent Morris Men with 'Invicta' at Folkestone International Folklore Festival (late 1960s)
Credit: Folkestone International Folklore Festival Archive courtesy of Folkestone Town Council

In 1964, while the Brown Horse was in Austria with the Handbell Hoodeners, the East Kent Morris Men made 'Invicta', their highly naturalistic white horse, which is still in use today (**25**). Their collection box can be dated before 1964 because it clearly represents the Brown Horse (**26**). However, East Kent Morris Men continued to use it for a long time after the Brown Horse's disappearance. A typed label on the underside of the box is almost certainly written by Barnett Field, who was known to have made a few collection boxes, and includes his particular phrase:

> "If ye the Hooden Horse do feed,
> Throughout the year ye shall not need."

 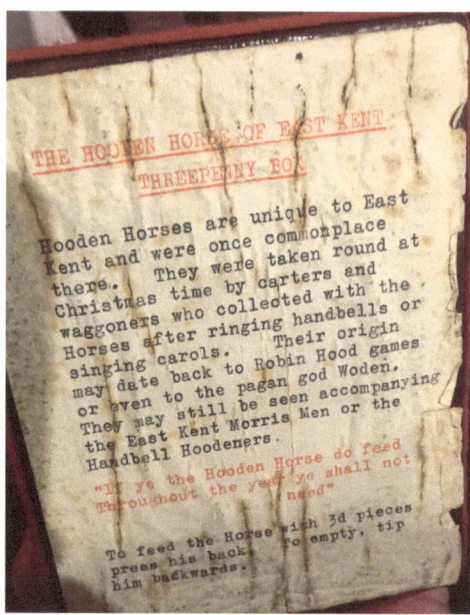

26 Hooden horse collection box, East Kent Morris (before 1964)
Aaron Janes Collection
Credit: James Frost

The Fields' creation and ongoing involvement in the Folkestone International Folklore Festival meant that hooden horses were kept in the spotlight, in particular the Brown Horse who was heralded as 'The Hooden Horse of Kent' in their publicity. In 1967 a 14-foot Giant Horse (**27–28**) was made for the festival, following the Boulogne giants' visits in 1963 and 1965. From photographs you can see what a close copy it is of the Brown Horse. It was made by Freddie Gosnold and Ray Strickland. Two operators sat, one above the other, controlling its four pneumatic tyred wheels and clacking its jaws. Its first outing was on the new National Folk Day, 1 May, instituted by the English Folk Dance and Song Society (Field and Field 1983, p.32).

27 The 'Giant Horse' at Folkestone International Folklore Festival (1971)
Credit: Folkestone International Folklore Festival Archive courtesy of Folkestone Town Council

28 The 'Giant Horse' at Folkestone International Folklore Festival (1980s)
Credit: Folkestone International Folklore Festival Archive courtesy of Folkestone Town Council

The image of the Brown Horse continued to have longevity on Hooden Horse pub signs around Kent. The first of these was the former Swan in Wickhambreaux, opened in 1956 by the Fields' personal network of folk groups: East Kent Morris, Ravensbourne Morris, the Handbell Hoodeners and the Folkestone National Folk Dance Group (Frampton 2018, p.119) (**29**). The Fields were buoyed up by this success and the following year established the first 'Hop Hoodening' event in and around Canterbury Cathedral (Field and Field 1983; Field 1967). The event is still going, with an interruption due to the COVID pandemic, and is attended by morris dancers, but it is now rare to see a hooden horse there. Many hooden horse themed pubs were consequently named by the Whitbread Brewery, both inside and outside of Kent. But, one by one, they have all changed or reverted to their previous names. Only the 'Hooden on the Hill' in Willesborough retained something of its hoodening association, fittingly becoming the 'Hooden Smokehouse and Cellar' after a fire in 2016 (Dover-Kent.com 2021). The Hungry Horse pub chain, unrelated to the 1950s revival, recently opened 'The Hooden Horse' at Westwood Cross, Thanet.

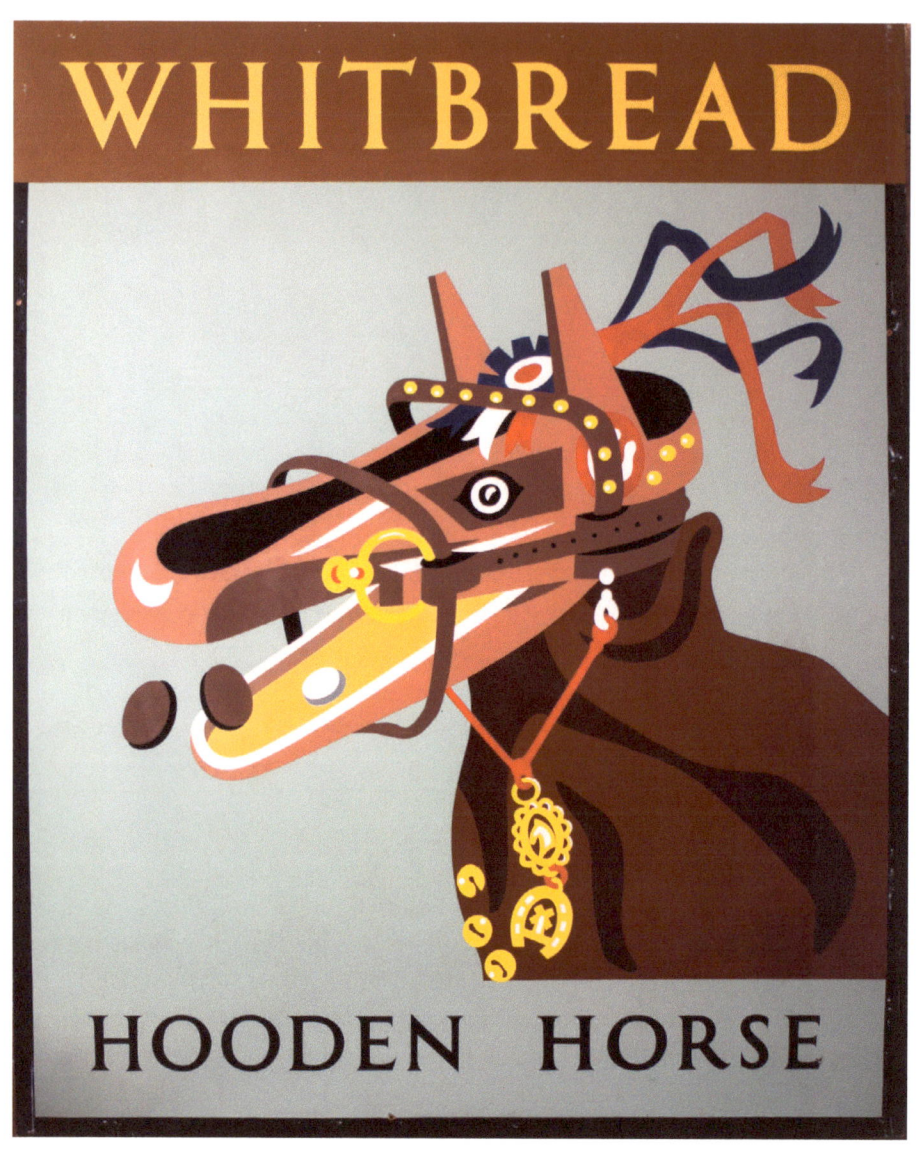

29 'Hooden Horse' pub sign, Wickhambreaux (1956)
John Field collection
Credit: James Frost

The revival of the hooden horse also took place where there were reports and memories of former teams, such as at Birchington in Thanet. The Birchington Townswomen's Guild horse (**30**) was made in 1954 for the Guild's Christmas revival and performed with them for a short period from 1955 to 1957 (Frampton 2018, pp.126–8). According to Barnett Field it was a copy of the old Walmer horse (**11**), but only resembles it in its trunk-like shape. The eyes and loose jaw movement makes it much more comical. This horse is also a good example of how much the custom was broadening its scope and appeal with an all-women hoodening team. Given the social context of hoodening outlined earlier, this would have been unlikely before the First World War. The horse was passed on to the St Nicholas Hooders in 2002 having been found in an attic by a Guild member. They added the current floral cover, as its previous one was lost. It became known as either Matilda or Edwina (after Edwina Curry).

30 Birchington Town Women's Guild hooden horse (1954)
St Nicholas-at-Wade with Sarre Hoodeners
Credit: James Frost

31 Edward Coomber's hooden horse (early 1950s)
Whitstable Hoodeners
Credit: James Frost

As with the work of the Fields, the revival at Whitstable was also led by the educated middle class, rather than the working class of the earlier tradition. Edward Coomber had a degree in Folklore Studies; having read Maylam he decided to revive hoodening, initially with schoolchildren, in the early 1950s. His green-coloured horse was made by the craft teacher at Sir William Nottidge School in Whitstable, Arthur Clark (**31**). The horse was kept in Coomber's garden shed in Nelson Road, Whitstable but was swept away in the floods in February 1953. It was rescued on the beach some weeks later, and now has oyster shells decorating its forehead to commemorate the event. The horse still has its original material, although this is now in a poor state of repair. Edward and Margaret Coomber took the horse out carol singing in Whitstable into the 1970s, ceasing when they reached retirement age. They would take it in turns to perform the horse or to lead it. The string for the jaw was operated by the Wagoner, outside the horse (Frampton 2018, pp.122–5). When Mark Lawson interviewed Coomber in 1980 he asked why the horse was green. One might expect an association with the green sea at Whitstable, but the reason was more prosaic. After the war there were shortages of many things including paint; as Clark had some green paint in his store at the school this was what was used (Lawson 2018).

Also on display in the exhibition are Coomber's own notes on hoodening inserted at the front of a copy of Percy Maylam's book. They read as follows:

[page 1]

<u>The Hooden Horse Party</u>
<u>Waggoner</u>
Top hat, whip, corduroys tied at clodhoppers, choker etc.
<u>Mollie</u> (man in woman's dress)
Besom, woman's clothes, bonnet etc.
<u>Jockey</u> (or Rider)
Small lightweight chap – jockey or similar cap
<u>Horse</u>
Strongest chap in the party –

All wear clodhoppers (ex army boots etc.) corduroy tied at knees, red spotted hanks or any appropriate farmyard workers' wear of the turn of the century

[page 2 is stamped at the top right corner: E Coombes, 12 High Street, Whitstable, Kent]

Xmas 1952

<u>Other Members of Party</u>
Carry lanterns, holly branches, musical "instruments" etc. carols

> Things desirable
> Lanterns on poles or branches
> Tambourine
> Drum
> Triangle
> Whistle or Recorders
> Rattle
> Holly Branches
> Melodeon, or Piano accordion, concertina
> Handbell ringers
> etc. etc.
>
> see Beaney Library Book "The Hooden Horse" by Maylam (1909)

The notes appear to be Coomber's plans for a first performance at Christmas 1952, as the parts, props, costumes, and instruments have not yet been allocated. He is keen to give the team an archaic or nostalgic feel, looking for farm workers' wear from the turn of the 20th century. In the final note we see that Coomber does not, at the point of writing, own a copy of Maylam. So the note was pasted into a copy of the book at a later date.

The Coombers' horse was passed on to Mark Lawson of the Whitstable Hoodeners. He recalls being both frightened and fascinated by a hoodening team in Whitstable in the late 1950s or early 1960s, at around the age of five and half. There was no scripted play but, as he recalled, the horse "snapped in my ear". Although Lawson recalls the horse being black rather than green his investigation turned up no other hoodening team than the Coombers' at that time. Lawson was a scout leader in the mid-1970s when he started his own team:

> …we used to go out carol singing and I thought it would be nice to take a hooden horse along. At that time, I still didn't know that it wasn't found everywhere. I assumed it was 'part' of Christmas – like robins and snowmen…This was in 1977. (Lawson 2018)

Lawson's new team, the Whitstable Hoodeners, were invited by Dixie Lee to take part in the Whitstable May Day festival in 1982 or 1983. As a result, they developed a hoodening play based on the Antrobus Souling play from Cheshire, along with local sayings and improvisation.

32 'Stinky', the Dead Horse Morris skull disguise (2003)
Aaron Janes Collection
Credit: James Frost

Along with the Whitstable Hoodeners, Lawson also founded Dead Horse Morris (named after the 'Burial of the Dead Horse' sea shanty) in Whitstable, 1986. Aaron Janes was a musician for both groups and in 2003 made a horse skull disguise from an Exmoor pony skull, inspired by the Welsh Mari Lwyd (see below) (**32**). The horse became known as 'Stinky', for obvious reasons. Dead Horse Morris are still active and hold another horse skull on a stick named 'Mitch', which is used more like a banner or trophy than a horse disguise.

The Whitstable May Day procession was revived by Dixie Lee (née Fletcher) in 1976. Lee had quickly become a lynchpin for folk activities in Whitstable since she moved there from Canada in 1969. She founded the Whitstable Folk Club in 1973, hosting acts like the Watersons, Peggy Seeger and Ewan MacColl. The Oyster Band was also formed by regular members of the club.

The May procession, with its Jack-in-the-Green, Robin Hood and Maid Marian (or alternatively, May King and Queen), had lapsed after the First World War. Lee's revival included those elements along with Wantsum Morris as dancers. One of their number, Jim 'the Ram' Bywater had been making jig dolls and similar objects. He suggested that he should make a hooden horse for the festivities (**33**), inspired by the hooden horses made for the Broadstairs Folk Week (**34**). The new horse, appropriately named 'Jim', appeared in the second May Day along with another animal disguise; the celebrated storyteller Taffi Thomas in a bear suit.

> He [Taffi Thomas] was an absolute bugger, he would get in people's cars, he would go right across them and get out the other door. He got on some bloke's motorbike and they tore off and came all the way back again. (Lee 2018)

Following that successful first event Oyster Morris was formed, initially with only women.

> After Taffi had done the bear stunt, we decided that because we had the Bear and Key [pub] in Whitstable we needed a bear. There was a picture of labourers waiting by Poverty Point being entertained by a dancing bear. So the bear has become part of the procession as well, because it's traditional. Then the other blokes who didn't play instruments wanted to dance as well so they formed the men's side. And that is how it all came into being.

33 Jim 'the Ram' Bywater's Whitstable May Day hooden horse (1976, repainted 2005)
James Frost Collection
Credit: James Frost

Oyster Morris became the lead side of the procession, with Dead Horse Morris as regular guests. Bywater's hooden horse fell out of use until 2006 when I started performing with it. The previous year I walked the procession with a tourney-type hobby horse (the sort you wear around your waist as if you were riding) of my own making. However, Lee found Bywater's old hooden horse Jim in her loft. It had suffered a lot of wear and tear and its jaw, which had been rigged with a bicycle break on a plumbing tube, was too stiff to operate. The plumbing tube was a clever device to catch money but the whole contraption made it much harder to handle than a traditional horse. I renovated it with new paintwork and a simple but effective snapping control on a rope, like the older examples.

The Jack-in-the-Green, Robin and Marian, Boris the Bear and myself as Jim the horse all continue to appear in Whitstable on the May Day Bank Holiday.

34 'Hobby' the horse, Broadstairs Folk Week
I.M.E. (Invictus Mugistis Equinus)
Credit: James Frost

The founder of Broadstairs Folk Week, Jack Hamilton, had a horse made for the festival in the 1960s but also occasionally borrowed the Chislet horse (Frampton 2018, p.76) (**7**). There is now a proliferation of twelve black hooden horses known as I.M.E or Invictus Mugistis Equinus who annually terrorize the town (**34**). On their website, Invictus Mugistis Equinus is "Latin-ish for 'undefeated horses neigh'" (2021).

The I.M.E. revel in the idea that they are performing illegally, since a ban on hooden horses in Broadstairs in the 1828 has never been lifted: Maylam (1909) reported on this incident, in which a woman was said to have been scared to death. After some investigation George Frampton located the event to a young pregnant woman, Susanna Crow, whose demise was apparently accelerated by her shock from encountering a "man dressed in a bear skin" (Frampton 2018, pp.40–1). Although Frampton wondered whether a hooden horse could had been mistaken for a bear skin, an actual bear disguise is likely enough. Whichever it was, the ban appeared to stand for all animal guising, and hooneners in the area ceased their activities for fear of prosecution:

> …after the Magistrates cried it down, they were afraid to go out with the 'hodenhouse' [sic] for fear they should fall into the hands of the 'patrols' and bosholders [officers]. (Maylam 1909, p.25)

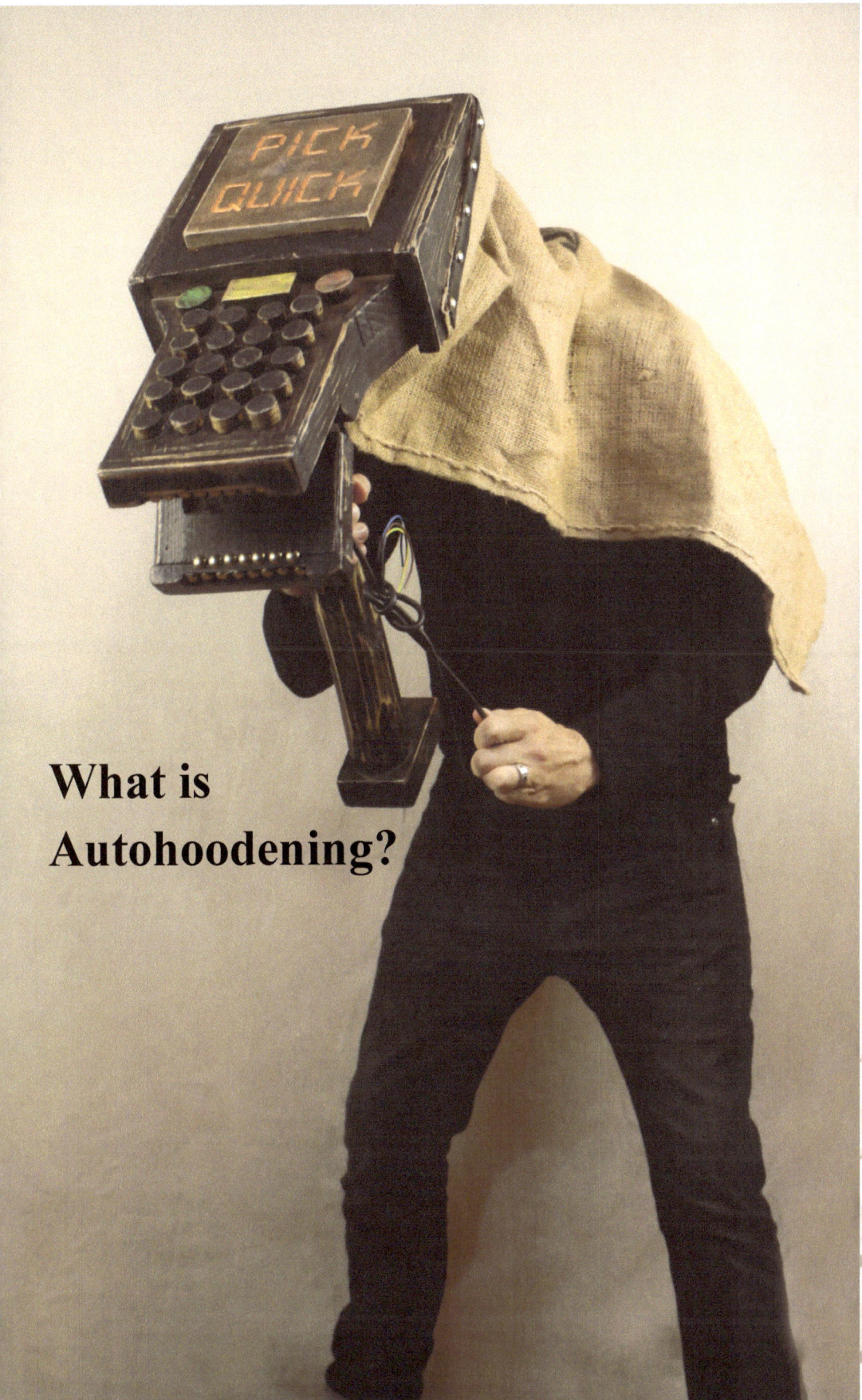

Image on preceding page:

35 Alexis the Warehouse Scanner (2020)
Post Workers Theatre
Credit: James Frost

Post Workers Theatre are comprised of Dash Macdonald, Nicholas Mortimer and Demitrios Kargotis. They describe themselves as:

> a design troupe investigating the future of politically engaged performance, reimagining historic forms of creative resistance for a contemporary context. PWT study and update historic workers theatre to address inequalities in the contemporary labour market and wider society, designing opportunities for workers and communities to discuss and challenge their conditions and imagine them otherwise...
> (Post Workers Theatre 2022)

Post Workers Theatre began investigating hoodening in 2019 as a way to connect seasonal folk performances with issues of contemporary seasonal work. Through visits to the Maidstone Museum archives, performances by the St Nicholas-at-Wade Hoodeners and the Canterbury Hoodeners, Post Workers Theatre gathered understanding and references to reframe hoodening to address precarious working conditions within 21st century platform capitalism.

36 Line Manager's costume (2020)
Post Workers Theatre
Credit: James Frost

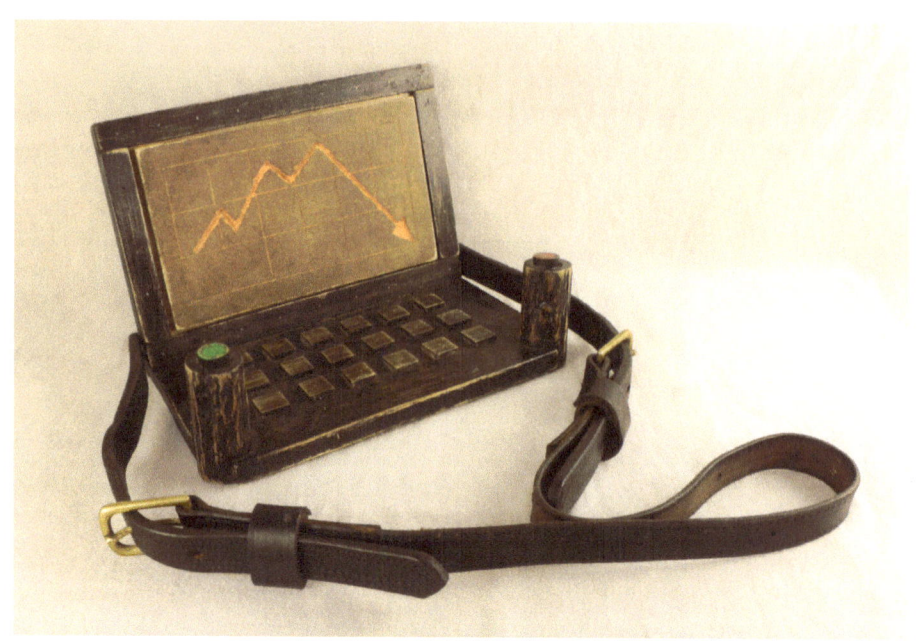

37 Line Manager's laptop (2020)
Post Workers Theatre
Credit: James Frost

Autohoodening started in 2019 as a symposium and workshop at Goldsmiths, University of London, which included guests Ben Jones, George Frampton and Doc Rowe. Post Workers Theatre describe Autohoodening as "a consciousness-raising custom for the age of Platform Capitalism."

Participants collectively wrote a scripted response to the format of folk plays that narrativized the experiences of seasonal Amazon staff. Drawing on worker testimony, interviews with GMB union managers and insights from guest journalist James Bloodworth who worked undercover in an Amazon fulfilment centre.

The event resulted in a performance of the new Hoodening play complete with a reworking of the song Poor Old Horse and prototyped cardboard costumes. In 2020, as part of the continuation of the project I made the following props for Autohoodening, on display in the exhibition:

- ALEXIS – a fusion of hooden horse and Amazon warehouse scanner, embodying the surveillance technology used by e-commerce (**35**).
- THE LINE MANAGER – a character, based on the Wagoner, who effectively enslaves the modern worker but is also enslaved by their laptop (**36–37**).

- THE MOLLY BOT – updating the Molly character into a much put-upon robotic shelving system who is under Alexis the scanner's spell.
- CAPTAIN SWING – inspired by the legendary icon of worker dissent in the English agricultural uprising of 1830 (**38**). His costume and head covering, influenced by English mummers and Irish 'straw boys', is made entirely from electrical wire. In his toolbox Swing has an array of computer bugs (**39**), ready to disrupt the automated workplace.

The play was developed in collaboration with Birmingham-based company Infinite Opera (**40**) and transformed into a full-scale opera with an original score written by Dani Blanco and additional hi-vis Picker and Packer costumes made by Lottie Wood. The opera fused wider folk components from Jack in the Green, Morris and maypole dancing that further developed narratives of death, resurrection and celebration.

38 Captain Swing's costume (2020)
Post Workers Theatre
Credit: James Frost

39 Captain Swing's computer bugs (2020)
Post Workers Theatre
Credit: James Frost

**40 Film still from *Autohoodening and the Rise of Captain Swing*,
Post Workers Theatre and Infinite Opera (2021)**
Credit: Andy Willsher and Iain Armstrong

Autohoodening responds to the context of traditional hoodening, before workers had rights or unions and where farm labourers' incomes were especially vulnerable during the winter. This paradigm is used to think about the precariousness of seasonal work and lack of union representation in modern workplaces such as Amazon.

> Autohoodening reimagines this custom for the age of automation, updating the characters, costumes, and performance to draw attention to the horrifying working conditions hidden behind consumer-facing infrastructure and the ease of 'one-click' delivery. Surveillance technology has become the evil antagonist, and fulfilment centre workers protagonists in a contemporary folk story of death and resurrection. (Post Workers Theatre 2022)

Autohoodening uses the visual and verbal prompts of folk drama to encourage a sense of community amongst contemporary workers, denied the right to unionize. Middle-class revival hoodeners sought to reflect the lives of working-class farm labourers and their horses, when that way of life had vanished; but perhaps they, like Autohoodeners, could see in hoodening a way of resisting creeping mechanization, dehumanization and a loss of cultural identity and memory after two world wars.

The Northern Beasts

Image on preceding page:

41 Skull horse from Richmond, Yorkshire (1956)
Credit: English Folk Dance and Song Society

At some point in the 20th century a horse skull was pulled out of the pond at Hooton Pagnell Hall near Doncaster, South Yorkshire (**42**). It had been thrown into the water by a troupe of mummers after their final performance, sometime in the 1880s. A spontaneous act perhaps, but one which resonates with ritual deposition practices in bodies of water around the British Isles. Greig (1988, p.157) associated the skull with the 'Old Horse' mumming tradition, in particular the 'Queen's Pony' team from nearby North Elmsall. Their play followed a pattern familiar in that region (pp.162–4): after a 'calling-on' song, the man wearing a horse disguise enters the scene and the Blacksmith is called upon to fit its shoe. After some comical slapstick, the horse falls limp and the Farrier is called to diagnose the problem. The horse is declared dead and is revived by the Farrier who forces it to swallow a ball (presumably a joke 'horse pill'). The Elmsall version of the play also included a 'Lady's Groom', but it is not clear what role they served. They may have led the Queen's Pony, like a Kentish Wagoner.

42 'Old Horse' skull disguise, retrieved from the pond at Hooten Pagnell Hall, Yorkshire (1880s)

Fred and Josh Mead Collection

Credit: James Frost

The deposition of the horse skull was seen by Greig less as a rite and more as a reflection of the changing circumstances of rural workers:

> One of the most poignant sights must have been the group of mummers who finally gave up their Christmas visits and in Hooton Pagnell, perhaps sadly, perhaps disappointed with poor receptions and meagre rewards, threw their Horse's head into the village pond, a gesture of finality…there was no-one left in the area who was willing to preserve a tradition which had ceased to fulfil its function in the community. (p.170)

After its recovery, the skull resided in Hooton Pagnell Hall until its recent sale by auction. The jaw is now stuck, but it has a handle on the back of its head for the purpose of snapping. Its front teeth are modelled from a kind of cement, also used to repair the damaged jaw. Its nose has been filled in with carved wood, presumably to appear more like a complete head than a defleshed skull, with two screws to hold it in place. The eyes are of blown glass. There is a cavity in the rear underside of the nose where a stick would slide in, making it into a mast-style skull disguise. However, there are no obvious fixings for ears. The skull, wood and cement material are all blackened but it's unclear whether this is paint residue, staining from smoke, or the result of sitting at the bottom of a pond for decades.

43 Skull horse from Richmond, Yorkshire (c.1880)
Credit: English Folk Dance and Song Society

One thing that is notable about the Old Horse mumming tradition in South Yorkshire is the variety of horse disguise constructions. Both wooden and skull heads were used. In the 1950s a team at Dore was known to have replaced their older wooden head with a skull. At Hoyland and Elsecar (of which a complete play survives) an actual horse's hide was used to cover two performers, who must have operated it like a pantomime horse. The disadvantage of this kind of disguise was that the back end of the horse would get kicked by rowdy audience members (Greig 1988, pp.156–8).

An 'Old Horse' mumming troupe from Richmond, near Sheffield, was photographed around the 1880s, some 23 miles from Hooton Pagnell (**43**). The horse is dark in colour, but its construction is difficult to determine. In a photograph of 1956, the stick at the front of the horse is thick and shaped like a hoof (**44**). In practical terms the stick needs to be strong to support the weight of a horse skull, whereas the hooden horse of Kent has a thinner stick to support a lighter head.

Also of note in the photograph are the blackened faces of the mummers, one of whom appears as a jockey; the other two are grooms in formal wear. We have discussed face-blackening before, in the section **What was Hoodening?** The little girl on the right is presumably an onlooker, rather than an acting member of the troupe.

Another important feature of the Old Horse custom was the close association with variations on Poor Old Horse song. Sometimes the song would be sung in full, with or without a play, and sometimes verses would be integrated throughout the play. Here is one version of the song:

> My clothing once was linsey-woolsey fine,
> My hair unlinkt and my coat it did shine.
> But now in open fields I'm forc'd for to go,
> To face the cold winter and the hailstorm and snow.
> Crying "Poor old horse, O poor old horse."
>
> My bait it once was of the best of hay
> That ever grew in fields or in meadows gay;
> But now to no such comfort I can get at all.
> I'm forced for the crop the short grass that grows upon the wall.
> Crying "Poor old horse, O poor old horse."
>
> My days are near an end, and now I must die
> And at some lownd dike back my weary bowk may lie;
> I do not greatly mind, for I'm clean done anyhow
> And my master does not care, for I'm worse than useless now.
> Crying "Poor old horse, O poor old horse."
>
> My skin unto the huntsman I freely do give
> My flesh unto the hounds I also bequeath

> Likewise my body stout, that's gone o'er so many miles
> Over hedge, over ditches, over gates and over stiles.
> Crying "Poor old horse, O poor old horse."
> (Stokoe 1899)

The story of the horse is truly tragic as he is devalued and forced to eat the "short grass that grows upon the wall". His fate is to be slaughtered for his hide and for meat. The imagery in the song bears a remarkable resemblance to a satirical verse written in the style of the Goliardic wandering monks around 1440. It begins:

> Middle English:
> Lyarde es ane olde horse, and may noght wele drawe,
> He salle be putt into the parke holyne for to gnawe;
> Barefote withowttyne schone, thare salle he goo,
> For he es ane olde horse, and may no more doo.
>
> Translation:
> Lyarde is an old horse, and may not well draw [i.e. draw a cart],
> He shall be put into the park holly for to gnaw;
> Barefoot without shoes, there shall he go,
> For he is an old horse, and may no more do.
> (trans. Reakes 1982)

Here we have a horse, who is past use and put to pasture, left to gnaw at holly, which I imagine to be worse than the "short grass that grows upon the wall". He is unshod, like the grumpy Old Horse who resists the Blacksmith. But there is more to this poem that might interest us.

Lyarde in Middle English means; 'a horse spotted with white or silver gray'; the name of a horse; the adjective for grey. But it is also an allusion to the Franciscan monks or Grey Friars. It refers at once to an elderly stallion, an impotent husband and aged Franciscan who can no longer fulfil his duties. The unshod horse also refers to the discalced or barefoot Franciscans (Reakes 1982 p.36). The poem mentions the large number of 'Lyarde's men', who are the many impotent hopeless husbands who fail to satisfy their wives – 'poor old horses' we could say. But, also, an unwelcome number of unchaste friars who wish to fulfil the husband's role. There is a great deal of word play and innuendo in the poem. Whether it is the source for the Old Horse song or not, we might wonder whether this analogy between an old horse and an old man was evident to the mummers. Certainly that connection was made in the 'Burial of the Dead Horse' sea shanty, mentioned earlier. Here are some potent selected verses for comparison:

A poor old man came riding by,
They say so, and they hope so,
They say, "Old man, your horse will die,"
Poor old horse!

If he dies, I will tan his skin,
They say so, and they hope so,
If he lives, I will sell him again,
Poor old horse!

[…]

From Ballycottin to Ballyack,
They say so, and they hope so,
Where I fell down and broke my back,
Poor old horse!

[…]

His old hide good leather will make,
They say so, and they hope so,
And his flesh salt horse for sailor's sake,
Poor old horse!
(Richards 1897 pp.281–4, Tangye 1883 p.22)

Like Lyarde and the Old Horse song, these verses indicate the hardship and grim fate of working horses. The analogy between the horse and old man no longer fit for work is made explicit (to the degree that the chorus is sometimes swapped for 'Poor old man!').

We can only wonder how much this analogy, which resonates through the centuries in literature and song, actually meant to the mummers at Hooton Pagnell as they sang the song and tossed their old horse into the pond. They were themselves retiring as mummers. What were they really putting to rest with this very provocative action?

44 'Lucky' the Wild Horse, Comberbach Mummers, Cheshire (1985)
Fred and Josh Mead Collection
Credit: James Frost

This mast horse from the Comberbach Soulcakers or Mummers is labelled 'Lucky, Nov 1985' on the inside (**44**), the year that the custom was revived there. In its original state we might imagine the Hooton Pagnell skull (**42**) to look like the horses of Richmond or perhaps those of modern Soulcaking groups in Cheshire. Like the Hooton Pagnell skull his nose cavity has been filled in and he has a handle on the upper part of the skull to snap the jaws. His leather ears and lolling leather tongue are tacked to the skull. He is painted in a red white and black colour scheme like a number of old hooden horses.

Horse disguises of this kind were taken on house-calling tours by Soulers or Soulcakers, on or after All Souls Eve, around Cheshire and Staffordshire. The players would perform variations of the mummers' hero-combat play, but usually with a horse sketch as part of a *quête* after the main play (a similar structure to that at Symondsbury, Dorset, **2**). The earliest known record of this tradition was noted by Ormerod in 1819: "Old Hob, or the custom of carrying a dead horse's head, covered with a sheet, to frighten people, is sometimes a frolic between All Souls Day and Christmas" (p.lii).

This regional custom has been variously known as the Wild Horse, Old Hob, Dick, Dicky Tatton, Dobby Horse or Young Ball. A skull head would be blackened, varnished and mounted on a pole with a sack or horse blanket covering the performer. Cawte (1978, p.125–6) notes a couple of instances, at Guilden Sutton and Huxley, where a wooden head was used. Like a hooden horse, these mast horses would often be decorated with ribbons and rosettes, suggesting a domesticated rather than 'Wild Horse' (that name perhaps indicates its ability to misbehave). Here is an excerpt from the play at Antrobus, two miles from Comberbach:

> Now ladies and gentleman just look around, and see if you saw a better class of beast on England's ground. He has a h'eye like a hawk, a neck like a swan, a pair of ears made from an old lady's pocket book, so read it if you can. Every time he opens his mouth his head's half off. Tell you what, if you look down his mouth you can see holes in his socks. Whoa stand still. He's a very fine horse, he's very fine bred. On Antrobus oats this horse has been fed. He's won the Derby, and the Oaks, and finished up pulling an old milk float. So stand round, Dick, and show yourself. Whoee, now stand still, stand still. (p.127)

This is a horse with a successful thoroughbred racing history (rather than a labouring one) but who has now, like Lyarde, passed his prime. The visual joke here is that the horse is usually made from a skull, so most definitely passed his prime a long time ago.

Cawte was keen to emphasize the ritualistic aspects of the custom, especially around the ceremonial act of burying the horse between seasons. This was observed at Frodsham and Higher Whitley, and possibly Alderley Edge. This seems to support the idea that there may have been some significance to throwing the skull in the pond at Hooton Pagnell as a final resting place.

45 'Old Tup', Handsworth, S. Yorkshire (c.1900)
Credit: English Folk Dance and Song Society

The Old Tup or ram animal disguise was traditionally found in the same area as the Old Horse customs, on the Yorkshire, Derbyshire, and Nottinghamshire borders near Sheffield. It is a mast style construction with the wooden head of a ram and clattering jaw, with the performer covered by a sack or sheepskin (**45**). Like hoodening it was a Christmas house-calling custom. As Greig (1988, pp.137–149) discusses, its entourage was exclusively boys between the ages of 10 and 13. The plays and song were passed down between peers. The tradition passed to the next generation when boys left school to start working, aged 14, when they might join an Old Horse team instead. Greig saw the young Tup teams as being like an initiation into the adult drinking culture.

46 The Comberbach Mummers' 'Tup', Cheshire (c.1985)
Fred and Josh Mead Collection
Credit: James Frost

The characters included a butcher, an old man or farmer character and an old woman 'Our Old Lass' (like the hoodeners' Molly), sometimes with a broom. The fact that pre-adolescent boys played the parts of old people added a comedic element, as in the negotiation for the Butcher's fee in one of the plays transcribed by Grieg (1988):

> What does he think I am, a bloody millionaire? I'm an old man tha knows, not a little kid. Tell him I'll give him another half and no more. (pp.187-188)

After the Tup has been praised for its largesse through song, it is killed by the butcher. The song continues explaining how various body parts will be used (like the 'Burial of the Old Horse' shanty):

> And all the men in Derby,
> Came begging for its eyes,
> To make a pair of footballs,
> For they were just the size,
> Singing fay lay, fay lay, fay lay nanny go lay.

> And all the women in Derby
> Came begging for its ears,
> To make a pair of aprons,
> To last them forty years,
> Singing fay lay, fay lay, fay lay nanny go lay.

In some cases a doctor is called to revive the Tup, as in hero-combat plays. These plays reflect the seasonal slaughtering practices of the local farming industry, but like the Old Horse and Lyarde poem, there may be other connotations about aging and usefulness in a small rural community.

The example exhibited is from the folk revival at Comberbach, Cheshire (**46**), from the same team as 'Lucky' the horse (**44**).

Image on preceding page:

47 Ben Edge, *The Mari Lwyd* (2018)
Private collection
Credit: Ben Edge

48 Mari Lwyd with carved wooden head, Glamorgan, Wales (19th century)
Credit: Horniman Museum and Gardens 15.2.50/1 © Heini Schneebeli

49 Mari Lwyd, possibly from Merthyr Tydfil (1929–1935)
Credit: James Madison Carpenter collection at the American Folklife Center, Library of Congress, Washington, D.C. Used by permission.

50 Mari Lwyd, Glamorgan, Wales (c.1920)
Credit: English Folk Dance and Song Society

The 'Mari Lwyd' of South Wales is usually a horse skull mounted on a pole with a covering for the performer. In preparation for making a Mari Lwyd, a skull would be buried for a time in fresh lime (Peate 1943, p.54–55). According to Cawte (1978, p.100), the head of the Mari Lwyd at Gower was buried and dug up the next year with mock gravity, much like the northern Old Horse custom.

The Horniman Museum's example from 19th century Glamorgan, is unusual in that it is carved from wood (**48**). At Tredegar in Monmouthshire, the head was also made from a block of wood (Peate 1943, p.54). Like the other horse disguises we have looked at, the Horniman example is decorated with ribbons and coloured rosettes. The plethora of rosettes engulfing most of the head is also seen in a number of early photographs in the National Museum of Wales. One of the Glamorgan songs accompanying the Mari praises its elaborate decorations:

> The fair folk [or fairies] of the household, come to the light without hiding, to see the wassail without pain, there's not one like it in Wales.
> It is an orchard of broad flowers, beautiful indeed and liveried, marvellous speckled ribbons have been tied into bows.
> It is a nimble comely mare; thousands praise her; her head is decorated with knotted strips. (trans. Owens 1959, pp.53–4)

The Mari Lwyd is a house-calling custom around Christmas and New Year. The team sings in Welsh at the threshold of the door to gain entry; there then ensues a back-and-forth singing match until the Mari is allowed in.

The earliest known description is from 1798:

> Another very singular custom [in North Wales] I never could learn the rationale of, is that of a man on New Year's Day, dressing himself in blankets and other trappings, with a factitious head like a horse, and a party attending him, knocking for admittance, this obtained, he runs about the room with an uncommon frightful noise, which the company quit in real or pretended fright; they soon recover, and by reciting a verse of some ancient cowydd, or, in default, paying a small gratuity, they gain admission. (J. Evans Letters cited in Peate 1943, p.55)

The comparisons with the hoodening Christmas house-calling should be obvious. The St Nicholas Hoodeners are recorded as having a 'knocker up' who would negotiate entry to a house, often by putting his foot, or the horse's stick through the door (Frampton 2018, p.62). Then, like the Mari team, they would rush in for horseplay, drinks and songs.

The companions to the Mari are the Leader, Sergeant or Corporal, the Merryman fiddler, Punch and Judy (with a broom, like Molly) and an Ostler (a role similar to the Wagoner of Kent) (Peate 1943, p.54; Owen 1959, p.54). On his travels around the UK in 1930s, the American folklorist James Madison Carpenter photographed a wooden Mari Lwyd with an Ostler (**49**). Rather than ribbons and rosettes, this horse wears a horse coat, making it more horse-like and less otherworldly than other examples (**50**).

The custom was also closely associated with Gwassailia or wassailing songs, some parties carried wassailing bowls with them. In Carmarthenshire the custom was known as Y Warsel, the wassail (Peate 1943, p.55–6). Some wassailing groups in Wales did not include the Mari Lwyd, but the performers had blackened faces and included Bessy, a man dressed as woman, who swept with a besom broom (Owens 1959, p.62).

Hoodening also seemed to have some associations with wassailing in parts of Kent. Wassailing is a widespread luck-bringing custom with its roots in the Anglo-Saxon *waes haeil* or 'be healthy' toast associated with the shared wassail cup. As well as being a house-visiting custom the wassail is also a field-visiting one, in particular the blessing of fruit trees (Simpson and Roud 2000, p.380). Hutton (1994, pp.13–14, 58) found wassailing bowls mentioned as early as the eighth century composition of Beowulf; its popularity in the Tudor court; and specific mention of a wassailing orchard in Fordwich, Kent, in 1585.

A variation on a well-known Sussex wassailing song was reportedly sung by hoodeners at Blean, Broad Oak near Canterbury and at Chestfield, Swalecliffe, in the latter part of the 19th century (cited above by Doel, and Maylam 1909, p.52). It is notable that these horse guising customs, on opposite sides of the country, should both have wassailing associations.

There has been some disagreement on the translation of *Mari Lwyd* amongst Welsh speakers, as this does not appear to be a native compound. *Mari* might be a colloquial spelling of the Holy Mary (whose festival was 3 February) or from the English 'mare', which seems likely given that Mari Lwyd is always referred to in feminine pronouns. *Lwyd* has some medieval precedents as 'holy', but as Owens (1959, p.56) points out is normally rendered as 'grey'. Notice the similarity between the Welsh *Lwyd* for grey and the Middle English *Lyarde*, an old grey horse. So we are left with either 'Holy Mary', based on medieval literary sources, or 'Grey Mare' based on English-derived words.

Mast horse disguises were also reported in Cornwall in the 19th century, but no images or examples of these seem to have survived. In local dialect the horse was called *Pen-glas* meaning 'grey head' – which is not all that far from *Mari Lwyd* or *Lyarde*.

The Pen-glas team would visit houses on Christmas day evenings in Penzance:

> A well-known character amongst them, about fifty years ago, was the hobby-horse represented by a man carrying a piece of wood in the form of a horse's head and neck, with some contrivance for opening and shutting the mouth with a loud snapping noise, the performer being so covered with a horse cloth, or hide of a horse, as to resemble the animal whose curvettings, biting, and other motions, he imitated. (Edmonds 1862, p.69)

The Pen-glas certainly sounds like the hooden horse and other mast disguises we have considered.

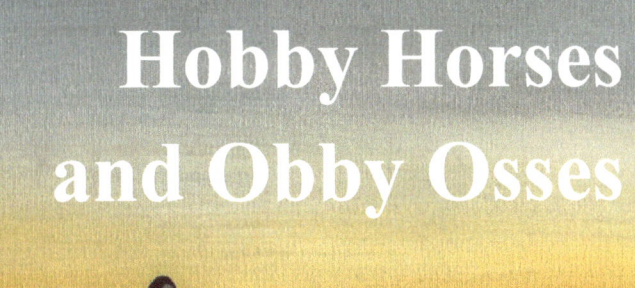

Hobby Horses
and Obby Osses

Image on preceding page:

51 Ben Edge, *The Obby Oss of Padstow* (2018)
Private collection
Credit: Ben Edge

As early as 1824, descriptions of the May Day Padstow 'Obby Oss' sound like its modern construction rather than a mast-style disguise (**51**). It is made "from canvas being extended with hoops, and painted to resemble a horse" (Hitchens and Drew 1824, p.720). The peculiarity of the Oss's construction confirms that the Cornish Pen-glas and Obby Oss are, at least from the mid-19th century, separate traditions. At Land's End the Pen-glas would capture girls under its skirt (Spooner 1958, pp.34–5), and it is this particular activity which it has in common with the modern Oss of Padstow.

Some of the earliest reports have the Oss drinking from 'Traitor [Treator] Pool' and drenching onlookers in muddy water (Hitchens and Drew 1824, p.720). The Padstow Oss is accompanied by a dancer with a painted paddle or club, called the 'teaser', who seems to coax the horse as he parades. Since the 1880s or 90s a similar 'Blue Ribbon Oss' has also paraded with its own team (**52**).

52 Blue Ribbon Oss and teaser, Padstow, Cornwall (May 1964)
Credit: Brian Shuel

The horse head of the Oss is now quite diminutive. In a drawing from around 1835 we see the hooped frame of the horse's body sitting on the shoulders of the performer with a distinctive head and large mask-head for the rider (**53**). The form of the horse has remained much the same but the horse's head and overall design is more stylized. Restoration of the 'Old Oss' in 1902 revealed that the horse's head once had 'snappers', along with a carved date of 1802 (Thurstan 1912, p.2). Like other guises we have looked at, the Oss is now coloured red, white and black. Apparently, the more abstracted design was inspired by a mask brought back by a sailor before 1865; this was confirmed by a member of the Brenton family who were regular performers (Rawe 1971, p.17).

53 May Day, Padstow (c.1835) – drawing reproduced in Thurston Peter's 'The Hobby Horse' (1913)
Credit: English Folk Dance and Song Society

Today, the Padstow Oss is a huge draw for tourists, with mementos like the exhibited model and commercially printed poster being popular (**54–55**).

Similar constructions to the Padstow Oss are found at Minehead in Somerset and Combe Martin in North Devon. There is some debate about whether the Padstow or Minehead May tradition is older: the earliest account at Minehead was performed by fisherman and sailors in 1830. Since World War I there have been two Minehead horses, the 'Minehead Horse' and the 'Sailors' Horse'. Their construction is much the same as at Padstow but with a heavier and narrower frame, they are also decorated with a profusion of ribbons on the upper surface and painted circular forms on the skirt (**56**). Until 1880 the wooden horse's head was covered in hare's skin and had a snapping jaw. It was accompanied by guisers with matching ribbons and conical hats known as 'Gullivers', which were revived in 1973 (Cawte 1978, pp.168–172).

54 Obby Oss souvenir model, Padstow, Cornwall (2002)
Fred and Josh Mead Collection
Credit: James Frost

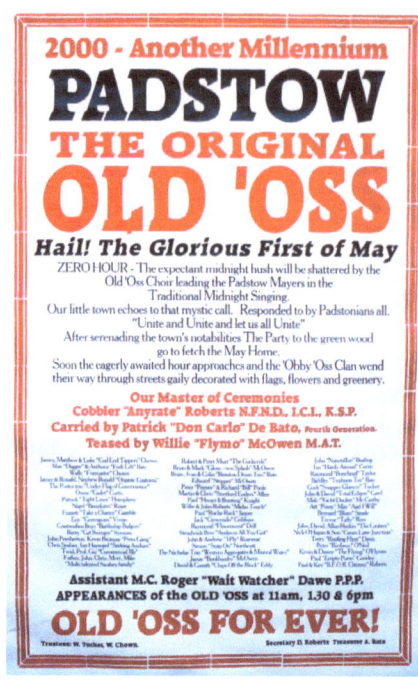

55 'The Original Old 'Oss' poster, Padstow, Cornwall (2000)
Fred and Josh Mead Collection
Credit: James Frost

56 Minehead Sailors' Horse (c.1948)
Credit: English Folk Dance and Song Society

57 Ben Edge, *Hunting of the Earl of Rone* (2020)
Private collection
Credit: Ben Edge

The 'hobby horse' of Combe Martin appears in the background of Ben Edge's painting (**57**), a section of whose skirt, which was in use until 2017, is in the exhibition (**58**). Until 1837 Combe Martin had a regular custom involving a hobby horse (of some kind), masked and covered in "gaily painted trappings", and a Fool character. The horse's snapping mouth was referred to as the 'mapper'. In the week before Ascension Day, in the Easter festive cycle, a group of 'Grenadiers' seek out the fugitive Earl of Rone, and fire a volley at him. The Earl character rides backwards on a real donkey, falls as if dead and is revived by the Fool. The Fool also uses a besom broom to splash water from a muddy puddle (echoing the Padstow Oss's antics) (Cawte 1978, pp.174–176). The custom was banned after 1837 because of "licentious and drunken behaviour" but was revived in 1974. The Earl is thought to be the 17th century Earl of Tyrone. The legend goes that he was captured in Lady's Wood, Combe Martin, then tried for treason and executed (Brown 1987, p.2). As the historical record is lacking on this, he may have just been a local criminal (p.6). In 1974 the revivalists looked to other West Country Osses for the design, Minehead being only twenty-four miles from Combe Martin (p.18).

58 Hunting the Earl of Rone hobby horse skirt, Combe Martin, Devon
Fred and Josh Mead Collection
Credit: James Frost

One of the more monstrous reinventions of the West Country Oss is Mark Norman's 'Black Dog Oss', reflecting his research into the folklore of spectral black dogs around the UK (**59**). It is based on the same kind of frame, sitting on the shoulders, but instead of a masked rider and horse's head it has an elongated dog head. In 1993 members of the Devon based Pennymoor Singaround folk group created an Obby Oss festival, "The Running of the Black Dog", which ran for around a decade.

59 Black Dog Oss, Devon (1993)
Mark Norman Collection
Credit: Mark Norman

The word Obby Oss is clearly a colloquial pronunciation of 'hobby horse' and applied specifically to the West Country shoulder-mounted framework. The word 'Hobby' is derived from the Old French word for a short-maned horse, *hobbin*. So a Hobby Horse is effectively a tautology: a 'horse horse'. Middle English spellings varied as *Hobyn*, *Hobin* and *Hoby*. The use of *Hobin* as a horse's name in Middle English easily became Dobbin, often applied to a cart horse (Skeat 1882). The English *Hobin* is also a variant of the French name Robin, an interesting connection, given the early associations between hobby horses and the Robin Hood games. Tantalizingly, this would mean that the name Robin Hood, can be rendered as 'horse covering' or conversely 'hooded horse'. The moment in the ballad *Robin Hood and Guy of Gisborne* when Robin dons Guy's horse-hide as a disguise is therefore a playful quip on his name (discussed in the section above, **What Was Hoodening?**). Whether this pun was evident to those participating in the Robin Hood games and plays is unknown. Certainly in the plays, the outlaw as a character is more important than the interesting etymology of his name.

60 Bidford Morris Dancers hobby horse (c.1900)
Credit: English Folk Dance and Song Society

The term 'hobby horse' has been used to refer to any kind of horse disguise or the child's mast-head toy. It is difficult to untangle any relationship between the various mast horses (documented from the 18th century) and the tourney horses (from perhaps the 16th), when the word 'hobby horse' is often used so freely. Often it refers to the kind of horse effigy that is worn around the waist as if the upper body of the performer is the rider, such as the Bidford Morris horse which, in a photograph from around 1900, is ridden by a performer in a military uniform. Notice the tiny legs dangling at the side of the horse's body (**60**). This type was referred to by Alford (1978) as the 'tourney' horse. The history of the tourney has been well documented by Alford, Cawte (1978), and Hutton (1994). By the late 16th century, it was widespread throughout England and would be found at May games alongside Marian, Robin and morris dancers; at midsummer parades and pageants; New Year festivities; municipal events; church fundraising; and accompanying itinerant performers.

61 Hobby horse detail from the 'Merry May' stained glass window, Betley Hall, Staffordshire (1621)
Victoria and Albert Museum
Credit: © Stuart Cox / Victoria and Albert Museum, London

One of the earlier representations of a tourney hobby horse is the 17th century stained-glass window celebrating May games, from Betley Hall, Staffordshire (**61**). It includes a scroll inscribed 'Merry May', morris dancers, a Maid Marian or May Queen, Friar Tuck, and a hobby horse. Wiles (1981, p.21–22) dated the style of costume between 1490 and 1520. Cawte (1978, pp.43, 58) explains the more puzzling details: the ladle in the hobby horse's mouth is for collecting money, and the "daggers in the nose" of the rider is a "method" or trick of the hobby horse dance, as mentioned in a contemporary play.

62 'Hob Nob', Salisbury, Wiltshire (c.1950)
Credit: English Folk Dance and Song Society

An early surviving example of a tourney horse is the 'Hobnob' of Salisbury (**62**). A hobby horse formed part of the City Corporation's Midsummer Eve parade and was first mentioned in records of 1572, along with Maid Marian's coat. The following century it was mentioned alongside the Salisbury Giant (St Christopher); both are now held in Salisbury Museum. The current head of the Hobnob is thought to be 17th century and can be operated to snap and move up and down and side to side (Cawte 1978, pp.29–35). Overall, the costuming of the Hobnob reflects the pomp and ceremony of its context.

63 Plough Monday hobby horse from Burringham, Lincolnshire (c.1920)
Credit: English Folk Dance and Song Society

Some hobby horses seem a long way from May Day and midsummer revelries. The horse disguise photographed at Plough Day at Burringham, Lincolnshire, is quite bizarre (**63**). It has a diminutive, almost phallic head (like an Oss), but the large horse-jacket with eye holes cut out of it makes it appear as a sinister horse-man hybrid; the stuff of folk horror. There are some confused accounts of the horse disguises of this region, often referred to as 'sieve horses', as they were made from farm machinery such as plough parts and sieves. According to Cawte (1978), there were memories of such beasts at East Butterwick (near Burringham) around 1830. Like other plough customs, the performers were farm labourers or horsemen. Their wooing plays (involving comedic suitors) often included Bet, a man dressed as woman sweeping with a besom broom (pp.133–8). We've already considered how the lives of 'Plough Boys' or 'Plough Jacks' might be considered analogous to that of the old hoodeners (in the section above, **What Was Hoodening?**).

Image on preceding page:

64 Ben Edge, *Abbots Bromley Horn Dance* **(2018)**
Private collection
Credit: Ben Edge

The horse may be the dominant form of animal guising in Britain since the Middle Ages, but during the medieval period it is the stag which appears most frequently. There is one such custom which survives to this day at Abbots Bromley, Staffordshire. It is performed on the Monday following 'Wakes Sunday' in September. It includes a tourney style horse and rider along with a group of dancers carrying reindeer antlers on poles. Although the antlers are used as a prop for dance, without a covering for the performer's body, the implication is that they represent dancing stags (**65**).

65 Abbots Bromley Horn Dancers (1963)
Credit: Brian Shuel

The Horn Dance remained a working-class practice when other customs like hoodening needed revival by middle class professionals after the social changes of two World Wars. Locals described the same working-class family, the Fowells, as leaders of the dance since the 18th century:

> In the 1970s, most of the dancers had not received full-time education beyond the age of sixteen and did not belong to the professional classes. […] attempts to control the Horn Dance by the established middle class and incoming middle class met with little success. (Buckland, 2001, pp.4, 8)

Certainly, during the 20th century the Fowells struggled with some performers going further afield for work and others having their pay cut for taking time out for the Horn Dance. As the then leader Alfred Fowell said:

> We were all poor then. All the chaps were poor. That's all I ever worried about. I used to worry about the money. As long as I had enough to pay those chaps it was all right, I didn't worry. (p.5)

Local tradition dictates that the antlers used in the dance, which are stored in the village church, are not to leave the parish. The artefact exhibited is one of six replicas commissioned by Commander E.H.M. Nicholson (chairman of the Sheffield branch of the English Folk Dance and Song Society), from George Bradbury; a wheelwright and joiner of Abbots Bromley. They were presented to the society in 1930 and are now kept in Cecil Sharp House, London (Art UK) (**66**).

In his *Natural History of Stafford-shire* (1686, p.434) Robert Plot described the performance. His description is recognizably the same form as the modern rendition, except that it took place at Christmas:

> At Abbots, or now rather Pagets Bromley, they had also within memory, a sort of sport, which they celebrated at Christmas (at New-Year, and Twelft-day) call'd the Hobby-horse dance, from the person that carried the image of a horse between his leggs, made of thin boards, and in his hand a bow and arrow, which passing through a hole in the bow, and stopping upon a sholder it had in it, he made a snapping noise as he drew it to and fro, keeping in time with the Musick: with this Man danced 6 other, carrying on their shoulders as many Rain deers heads, 3 of them painted white, and 3 red, with the Armes of the chief families (viz. of Paget, Bagnot, and Wells) to whom the revenews of the Town cheifly belonged, depicted on the palms of them, with which they danced the Hays, and other Country dances.

Even earlier, in 1532, a payment to the Abbots Bromley 'hobby-horse', "just as the customary dues have been from ancient time", was found in court proceedings (Heaney 1987, p.359). The antlers themselves have an even more ancient provenance. In 1976 one set of antlers were carbon-dated by Theresa Buckland (1980) to the year 1065, give or take 80 years. Being extinct in the British Isles, these reindeer may have originated in Scandinavia.

By at least 1893 the custom had moved to the beginning of September. It included a character separate from the hobby horse, referred to as Robin Hood, now holding the percussive bow and arrow, along with a man as Maid Marian and a Fool (Cawte 1978, pp.69–72) (**67**). So at some point, if not originally, the custom became associated with the highly popular and widespread Robin Hood games, mentioned earlier.

66 George Bradbury's replica of an Abbots Bromley Horn Dance antler head (c.1929–1930)
English Folk Dance and Song Society
Credit: James Frost

The costumes varied from the late 18th to early 20th century, conforming to various ideals of rural antiquity, until settling into the current pattern. This is supported by Buckland's (2001, p.3) observations that the performers were aware of the national and foreign interest in their custom since Plot's account, and would actively promote theories of their antiquity as a supposed pagan fertility rite. However, the main character motifs of the stags, the bow and arrow and mounted horseman seem to directly signify hunting.

67 Abbots Bromley Horn Dancers, Staffordshire inc. hobby horse, Fool, Maid Marian and Robin Hood (c.1890)
Credit: English Folk Dance and Song Society

The fact that the antlers are still being used in performance, some 900 years or more after the reindeer were alive, is fairly staggering, given the poor condition of some animal disguises only 70 years after their construction (e.g. Edward Coomber's hooden horse). It certainly leads to the question of whether they once formed a more complete mast-style disguise with a covering, perhaps an animal hide.

A reference to a stag disguise appears in Shakespeare's *As You Like It* (act IV scene II), when the character Jaques refers to one of the foresters who has killed a deer:

> …it would do well to set the deer's horns upon his head for a branch of victory. Have you no song, forester, for this purpose? […]
> What shall he have that kill'd the deer?
> His leather skin and horns to wear.

This is often considered a stage direction for a slaughtered deer, but Latham (1975, p.103–104) points out how the "text seems to call rather for antlers, in the style of the Abbots Bromley Horn Dance". Hutton (1994, p.48) drew comparison between these verses, the Horn Dance, and a traditional bearing of antlers to mark the end of a successful hunt at Tutbury Priory near Abbots Bromley.

In *The Merry Wives of Windsor* (act IV scene IV) Falstaff is persuaded to disguise himself as Herne, wearing a stag's antlers in Windsor Park at midnight:

> Mrs Page. There is an old tale goes that Herne the hunter,
> Sometime a keeper here in Windsor Forest,
> Doth all the winter-time, at still midnight,
> Walk round about an oak, with great ragg'd horns;
> And there he blasts the tree and takes the cattle
> And makes milch-kine yield blood and shakes a chain
> In a most hideous and dreadful manner:
> You have heard of such a spirit, and well you know
> The superstitious idle-headed eld
> Received and did deliver to our age
> This tale of Herne the hunter for a truth.

And alternate lines, likely inserted by a different author:

> Oft haue you heard since Horne the hunter dyed,
> That women to affright their little children,
> Ses that he walkes in shape of a great stagge... (Oliver 1971, p.118)

The verses refer to the folk legend of Herne, the former forester who hung himself from a tree. An oak in Windsor Park (which has since been felled) was even known as 'Falstaff's Oak' and 'Herne's Oak' (Simpson and Roud 2000, pp.174–175). Herne is said to haunt Windsor Park, mounted on a black horse and with a head of stag's antlers. Foresters who have been damned are said to serve Herne in his nightly hunts (Marshall 1981, pp.119–124).

Falstaff's disguise is intended as mockery, for he is planning to cuckold others, i.e. 'wear the horns'. This notion evokes a few instances of animal guising used in mockery customs. Lowsley (1888) reported on the custom of the Hooset Hunt, in the same county of Berkshire. The Hooset was "a horse's head drest up", sounding much like a mast disguise (p.8).

> When persons are believed to be guilty of incontinence, men and boys assemble for a "Hooset Hunt," they take with them pots or pans or anything wherewith to make a discordant noise, and this they call "Rough Music," they also carry the "Hooset" on a pole. On arrival at a house to be visited, the "Rough Music" is vigorously played, and the "Hooset" shaken in front of all the windows, and even poked into them if any be open. (p.92)

No Hooset has survived, but it is clearly related to the 18th century Wooset or 'ooset' of neighbouring Wiltshire, also a mocking or chastising procession with rough music, in which the subject of the mockery was placed backwards on something like a mast horse or stag head (Thompson 1991, p.471).

Cawte (1978, p.192) discussed this kind of disguise of a horse's head, sometimes with additional horns, in Hampshire, Wiltshire and Wales, comparing it to the French shaming custom known as *Charivari*. In Devonshire he describes a stag hunt where a man with horns and painted face was hunted by men acting as huntsman and hounds. The mock kill, using a bladder of ox blood, would take place at the house of an adulterer as a gesture of shame. The shaming ritual associations of a hunt, and riding backwards on a beast of burden, may provide us with a more fitting explanation of the Hunting of the Earl of Rone than the search for a historical Earl. And if it seems we have moved a long way from Kentish hoodening, it is worth highlighting a seemingly unique practice in Challock known as 'tin-canning' that included a hooden horse. Frampton (2018, p.80) recorded this testimony in 2000:

> My father [Owen Hams] was very vague [about the hooden horse usage in Challock]. It had become discredited and it was almost swept under the carpet. People got it out or were said to have done in the 1880s or 1890s. It was used at the time for shaming people, like if somebody was living with somebody they shouldn't – this thing was paraded.

A similar practice was also known as 'sweeping out' at St Nicholas-at-Wade, which might refer to the removal of rubbish from the community or the actions of the Molly character with or without a hooden horse (pp.80–81).

These associations are promising and might help tie together some disparate practices and types of animal disguise into a network of related social customs. But as Owen Hams's testimony shows, such practices were not discussed outside of the tight social group and certainly not to prying antiquarians and anthropologists of a different social strata.

Returning to the earlier context of the Abbots Bromley antler heads, it is worth considering that at least in continental Europe mast- or even hooden-style stag disguises certainly did exist in the late Middle Ages. In the bottom marginalia of a manuscript of the *Romance of Alexander* is a depiction of a mast disguise of the kind we are familiar with (**68**). It is being played to, or 'teased', by a musician. This is one of many different illustrations in the manuscript of animal guises, animal-human hybrids, performing animals and people largely superfluous to the narrative. The manuscript is a rich source of visual information on performative practices in the 14th century and was used as such by Strutt (1801), Alford (1978) and others. The manuscript was illustrated by the Flemish illuminator Jehan de Grise from 1338–1344. The marginalia evoke the popular entertainments of the *festes* of Northern France and the Low Countries around the 13th to 15th centuries, but they may also have been recognizable to the English who acquired the manuscript as spoils from the Hundred Year War, around 1410 (Cruse, 2011).

68 Stag disguise marginalia in the *Romance of Alexander* (1338–1344)
Credit: Photo Bodleian Libraries. MS Bod. 264.

Maylam (1909 p.87) himself noticed the similarities between disguises in the *Romance of Alexander* and the hooden horse. He saw these as evidence that the hooden horse was a crude, primitive form of animal disguise. But that doesn't sit well with his assertion that the hooden horse is also a degenerated form of tourney-type or West Country hobby horse. Either the hooden horse is a survival of the primitive medieval stag disguise or it is a degeneration from the more courtly hobby horse, but it is difficult to see how it could be both. Alford (1978 p.30) also felt the 'skull and pole' was a 'primitive type' of hobby horse. For her, animal guising provided a social function:

- Opportunity to collect food, drink and money
- Small group cohesion
- Continuation of tradition

So far, this is consistent with the customs we have been considering from the 18th century onwards. But she also proposed three possible explanations which we might consider hypotheses for the customs as survivals:

- Spirit of the season i.e. Midwinter
- Slaughtering custom
- Hunting custom

However, there is a problem with this search for origins: it is seemingly impossible to demonstrate an unbroken tradition which clearly began with a single motivation. It is not a simple case of tracing a line backwards like a family tree. Of course, as I hope to have demonstrated, the picture of cross-influence and cross-fertilization between customs is more complex and interwoven.

In trying to trace such a line, much has been made of the proclamations of early church fathers against animal guising. These tended to be directed at midwinter festivals, in particular the Roman midwinter festival of Kalends. Chambers (1903b) reproduces some thirty-five of them across Europe, between the second and eleventh centuries.

The surviving English proclamations come from the seventh century. St Aldhelm (also spelt Aldhem, Aldelm, Aldem, Eadhelm, Ealdhelm) in 685 referred to the temples of "unspeakable animals", especially stags (*ermuli cervulique*) who had been worshipped in "profane stupidity" (p.302). The Latin seems to have suffered from poor transcription, or idiosyncratic phrasing. Clearly he is referring to animal cults or the worship of deities in the shapes of animals but is not clear whether we can infer an animal disguise, as is the case with the Roman Kalends in continental Europe. The passage led to Chambers theorizing that it referred to the Celtic Cernunnos (often associated with Herne and the Wild Hunt):

> ... a cervulus or 'hobby-buck' rather than a 'hobby-horse' is prominent with the widespread worship throughout the districts whence many of these notices come of the mysterious stag-horned deity, the Cernunnos of the Gaulish altars. (1903a, pp.258–259)

There are at least three centuries between St Aldhelm's proclamation and the earliest possible construction of the Abbots Bromley antler heads, so it is impossible to say if there is a connection. But this does indicate a consistent human urge to disguise as an animal for one purpose or another.

Even more historically remote are the skull disguises made from red deer and found at Star Carr in Yorkshire (**69**). These are some 11,000 years old, from the Mesolithic era. They are carefully shaped with drilled eye holes. They may have been trophies, part of a hunting ritual or of shamanic practice. The latter seems likely, given recent analysis and comparison with analogous cultures (Little et al 2016).

There is no way of telling whether these enigmatic artefacts are the origin of any surviving customs, especially as we can't say for certain their social or religious function. Given the many migrations of people during and since the Mesolithic period we can't even say whether they belong to the same ethnic peoples who frustrated the church fathers so much, so remote are they from that time. What they do tell us is a human need to identify with an animal through costume and mask.

69 Star Carr frontlets (c.9000 BCE)
University of Cambridge Museum of Archaeology and Anthropology
Credit: Reproduced by permission of University of Cambridge Museum of Archaeology & Anthropology 1953.61.A

What do animal disguises say about our relationship with animals?

Mostly, the old hoodening custom reflected an agricultural culture and community where the utilitarian workhorse was central. But also the horse was celebrated, decorated in trappings as if at a fair, ploughing competition, or country show. It was an object of pride, but sometimes abused by a clumsy rider. The horse toured its immediate community at Christmas, a time of precarious existence for those workers. It was symbolic of the lives of the performers themselves.

The revival of the hooden horse was part of a much larger revival of English folk song and dance. The folk revival attempted to capture the spirit of the working-class performances of the Victorian era, but driven by the educated middle class. As Boyes (2010 p.4) pointed out, it had "interventionalist intent…to effect a cultural change". We have seen an active movement to preserve the hoodening tradition as a Christmas house-calling custom (by the teams at Whitstable and St Nicholas-at-Wade), but we have also looked at the attempts to revive the hooden horse within other contexts (particularly led by the Fields, Coombers and morris dancing sides).

After each World War, folk revivals had a renewed purpose to preserve that which was threatened and find a shared culture. As we have seen, much of the rehabilitation of the hooden horse has been through summer festivals, which create community cohesion and a picture of the rural English idyll. Here, the horse often walks upright as a dancer, rather than as the bent over and weary workhorse of the Christmas tradition. In the revivalist movement there is something of the Frazerian romanticization and nostalgia for a lost and more primitive state of being, in the face of fast-moving industry and technology. The 'folk' and their culture are 'the other', somehow unaffected by modern change but perpetually facing extinction because of it: "…and without the notional existence of the rapidly disappearing Folk, there would be no rationale for a folk revival" (Boyes 2010, pp.17–18). But paradoxically, how can you revive a tradition or culture when its context and 'folk' have clearly disappeared? It can only ever be a construction, as Brocken (2003) stated in relation to folk music and dance: "…the eternal contradiction of revivalism: in order to popularize some kind of tradition one has to recontextualize it" (p.8).

For the folk revival, the hooden horse became a source of nostalgia, and an attempt to reconnect with a fast-disappearing way of life. But the hooden horse was also rediscovered as a mischievous entity in its own right, an unsettling presence that could disrupt the summer festival or question the precarity of the modern workplace.

Even if we accept hoodening in the latter part of the twentieth century as a middle-class construction or recontextualization, and the 'folk' as a rural fantasy, the custom still has great value as a dramatic form. Performing as a hooden horse can still feel vital, engaging, participatory and sometimes quite primal. Post Workers Theatre turn these drives towards social criticism in the digital age.

The horse disguises of Cheshire and the rural area to the north east of Sheffield, along with the Derby Tup, reflect an animal abused and worked to death, or slaughtered for meat. This is enhanced by the songs of those regions, and their literary allusions. It is also a metaphor for the performers' own working lives. The Welsh Mari Lwyd shares these associations, but is often seen now as a spirit of the season. Although in broad terms we find skull disguises in Wales and northern England and wooden heads in the south, there are a handful of reports that contradict this assumption, to the degree that it is impossible to say whether the skull or wooden head is indeed indigenous to a particular region. However, we are getting a picture of wide-ranging horse disguising customs across the UK with some striking similarities: the construction of the horse; the attendant characters; the house-calling customs; and associations with other customs like wassailing.

Very different in significance is the tourney type of hobby horse. It represents a horse being ridden, or the horse and rider as one. A horse might be ridden for leisure, warfare or to hunt. From its earliest reports this kind of hobby horse was seen in the context of a courtly or municipal entertainment. It is transport for the kind of activity that might involve the elite soldiery or aristocracy: the horse elevates and ennobles its rider. Unlike the hooden horse which throws its rider, the hobby horse is tamed, controlled and civilized. Did the strange dimensions of the West Country Oss evolve from the more widespread tourney hobby horse? Its behaviour is more like the mischevious mast-horse, but we can wonder whether the purpose of the Padstow 'teaser' is intended to tame or torment it.

The stag disguise represents an animal that is wild and untameable: an animal that is hunted. The strange and intriguing connections between horse and stag disguises in shaming customs are surely also about the process of taming and civilizing behaviours in small communities.

All these different modes of disguise are about how we relate to animals, in particular our close historical relationship with horses. But they might also tell us something about ourselves, as metaphors for our wildness or civilization, potency or impotence. We are, after all, animals and still capable of behaving as such.

Bibliography

Alford, V. (1978) *The Hobby Horse and Other Animal Masks*. London: Merlin Press.

Anon. (15th century) 'Lyarde', in Wright, T. and Halliwell, J.O. (eds) (1843) *Reliquae Antiquae Vol.II,* London: John Russell Smith, pp.280–282.

Art UK (no date) *Abbots Bromley Horn Dance Antlers: George Bradbury (active 1929–1930)*, available at: https://artuk.org/discover/artworks/abbots-bromley-horn-dance-antlers-249031

Bond, K. (2022) email to James Frost, 8 October. [Bromley Historic Collections]

Boyes, G. (2010) *The Imagined Village: Culture, ideology and the English Folk Revival.* 2nd edn. Leeds: No Masters Co-operative Ltd.

Bracey, A. (2017) email to James Frost via Samantha Harris, 7 September. [Maidstone Carriage Museum]

Brocken, M. (2003) *The British Folk Revival 1944–2002.* Farnham: Ashgate Publishing Ltd.

Brown, T. (1987) *The Hunting of the Earl of Rone*. Combe Martin: Earl of Rone Council.

Buckland, T. (2001) 'Dance, Authenticity and Cultural Memory: The Politics of Embodiment', in *Yearbook for Traditional Music* 33, pp.1–16

Buckland, T. (1980) 'The reindeer antlers of the Abbots Bromley Horn Dance: a re-examination' in *Lore and Language* 3(2) part A, pp.1–8.

Cawte, E.C. (1978) *Ritual Animal Disguise: A Historical and Geographical Study of Animal Disguise in the British Isles.* Cambridge: D.S. Brewer Ltd.

Chambers, E.K. (1903a) *The Mediaeval Stage: Vol. I*. Oxford: Oxford University Press.

Chambers, E.K. (1903b) *The Mediaeval Stage: Vol. II*. Oxford: Oxford University Press.

Cruse, M. (2011) *Illuminating the Roman d'Alexandre: The Manuscript as Monument.* Cambridge: D.S. Brewer.

Dover-Kent.com (2021) *Kent's Public House Archive*, available at: http://www.dover-kent.com/

Edmonds, R. (1862) *The Land's End District*. London: J. Russell Smith.

Field, B. (1967) 'The Hooden Horse of East Kent', in *Folklore* 78, p.203–6.

Field, B. and Field, O. (1983) *Midsummer Fire: The Story of The Folkestone International Folklore Festival 1961–1981.* Hythe: Schlupfwinkel.

Frampton, G. (2018) *Discordant Comicals: The Christmas Hoodeners of East Kent, Tradition and Revival.* 2nd edn. St Nicholas-at-Wade: Ozaru Books.

Frampton, G. (1995) 'The Return of the Hooden Horse', in *Bygone Kent* 16(12), Dec 1995, pp.743–748.

Grieg, R. (1988) *Seasonal House-Visiting in South Yorkshire*. MPhil thesis, University of Sheffield.

Grove, L.R.A. (1956) 'Researches and Discoveries in Kent: Wingham District.' *Archæologia Cantiana* 70, p.273.

Heaney, M. (1987) 'New Evidence for the Abbots Bromley Hobby-Horse', in *Folk Music Journal* 5 (3), pp.359–60.

Hitchens, F. and Drew, S. (eds) (1824) *The History of Cornwall: Vol. I*. Helston: William Penaluna.

Hugill, S. (1969) *Shanties and Sailors Songs*. New York: Praeger Publishers.

Hutton, R. (1994) *The Rise and Fall of Merry England. Oxford: Oxford University Press*.

Invictus Mugistis Equinus: A Hooden Horse Site (2021) available at: https://hoodenhorse.co.uk/

Jones, B. (2019) *Hoodening Website*. http://www.hoodening.org.uk/

Jones, B. (2018) Interview with James Frost, 24 July.

Latham, A. (ed.) (1975) *The Arden Shakespeare: As You Like It*. London and New York: Methuen.

Lawson, M. (2018) Interview with James Frost, 8 March.

Lee, D. (2018) Interview with James Frost, 25 July.

Little, A. et al (2016) 'Technological Analysis of the World's Earliest Shamanic Costume: A Multi-Scalar, Experimental Study of a Red Deer Headdress from the Early Holocene Site of Star Carr, North Yorkshire, UK', in *PLOS ONE* available at https://doi.org/10.1371/journal.pone.0152136

Lowsley, B. (1888) *A Glossary of Berkshire Words and Phrases*. London: English Dialect Society.

Marshall, S. (1981) *The Book of English Folk Tales*. London: Duckworth.

Maylam, P. (1909) *The Hooden Horse, An East Kent Christmas Custom*. Canterbury: Percy Maylam.

Oliver, H.J. (ed.) (1971) *The Arden Shakespeare: The Merry Wives of Windsor*. London and New York: Methuen.

Ormerod, G. (1819) *The History of the Palatine and City of Chester, Vol.I*. London: Lackington, Hughes, Harding, Mayor and Jones.

Owen, T.M. (1959) *Welsh Folk Customs*. Llandysul: J.D. Lewis and Sons Ltd., Gomerian Press.

Parish, W.D. and Shaw, W.F. (1888) *A Dictionary of the Kentish Dialect and Provincialisms in use in the County of Kent*. Lewes: Farncombe & Co.

Peate, I.C. (1943) 'Mari Lwyd: A Suggested Explanation', in *Man* 43, pp.53–58.

Plot, R. (1686) *The Natural History of Stafford-shire*. Oxford.

Post Workers Theatre (2022) *Post Workers Theatre website*, available at: https://www.postworkerstheatre.com/about

Rawe, D.R. (1971) *Padstow's Obby Oss and May Day Festivities*. Padstow: Lodenek Press.

Reakes, J. (1982) '"Lyarde" and Goliard', *Neuphilologische Mitteilungen* 83(1), pp.34–41.

Richards, E.A.M. (1897) 'Ancient Custom at Sea', in *Folklore* 8(3), pp.281–4.

Romance of Alexander (1338–1344) Bodleian Libraries, MS Bod. 264, University of Oxford.

Simpson, J. and Roud, S. (2000) *A Dictionary of English Folklore*. Oxford: Oxford University Press.

Skeat, W.W. (1882) *An Etymological Dictionary of the English Language*. Oxford: Clarendon Press.

Small, J. (1976) *The Hooden Horse: An East Kent Custom*. Deal: Maritime and Local History Museum. [pamphlet]

Spooner, B.C. (1958) 'The Padstow Obby Oss', in *Folklore* 69, pp.34–38.

Stokoe, J. (1899) *Songs and Ballads of Northern England*, London and Newcastle-upon-Tyne: Walter Scott Ltd.

Strutt, J. (1801) *Sports and Pastimes of the People of England*. London: Methuen & Co.

Tangye, R. (1883) *Reminiscences of Travel in Australia, America, and Egypt*. London: Sampson Low, Marston, Searle, & Rivington.

Thomson, E.P. (1991) *Customs in Common*. Pontypool: Merlin Press.

Thurstan, P. (1912) *The Cornish Obby Oss*. Monmouth: Oakmagic Publications, 1997.

Tillis, S. (1999) *Rethinking Folk Drama*. Westport, Connecticut: Greenwood Press.

Wiles, D. (1981) *The Early Plays of Robin Hood*. Cambridge: D.S. Brewer.

MY LIFE AS A HOODENER

George

My name is George, and I'm a Hoodener. Some would qualify that as "a St Nicholas-at-Wade with Sarre Hoodener", but for us, we're simply "The Hoodeners", just as most tribes refer to themselves with words meaning simply "people". It's only outsiders who need to make distinctions. At times I'm also known as Ben Jones – linguist, publisher, musician, gorilla fundraiser, cubist – but all of those are irrelevant today.

Identity is a strange thing. It emerges in war, at the death of a monarch, at a football match, in a choice of clothes or which pub one drinks at. Being a hoodener is a powerful part of my personal identity. But what does that mean?

I saw the light of day in June 1966, as did Dobbin, after a few decades of slumber. He was not woken from his rest by the World Cup celebrations, but by my father. My brother Adam became a hoodener that year. Over the years, my other brother and my mother occasionally joined the team too, and my sister Mala similarly performed an ancillary role with the carol singers who accompanied the hoodening. Our house was one of the few venues that hosted a hoodening party every year; it has been the rehearsal venue since as long I can remember; and ever since Dobbin was given to my father in 1972, he and his companion horses have been stabled with us. I myself first took an active role in 1977, and my children in turn in the early 1990s. I have performed, I have written Hoodening scripts and songs (and a short story), I have published books and given talks about the tradition, I run the hoodeners' website and other social media, I am the only person to have retraced the Great Walk.

Does this make me uniquely qualified to write about hoodening? In a way it does, of course, even though there are others with similar claims and differing viewpoints. But in another way, it throws up obstacles.

Dead traditions are comparatively easy. You examine the relics in museums or archives, you analyse, you theorize and maybe produce a learned tome pronouncing what the essence of the tradition was. New evidence and insights may sometimes cast doubts on your theses, but most of the accepted knowledge is indisputable and immutable.

Living ones are more problematic. Having also spent many years in the martial arts, I am used to seeing criticisms that some are not 'traditional' because they change things. Stephen Hayes once wrote something like, "the most traditional thing I could do as a Ninja is NOT run around in straw sandals wielding a horsehair rope". So too with hoodening. We keep some things, we discard others.

Yet one cannot deny the past. If a researcher such as George Frampton, Geoff Doel or James Frost says "hoodeners: agricultural labourers", should I in good faith correct them by adding "and also monumental masons, bank clerks, polymer operatives, software engineers, professors of African history and Japanese interpreters"? Am I entitled to call activities some describe as hoodening "inauthentic", on the grounds that they take place outside East Kent and/or outside the season, repeat the same scripts every year, involve dancing, stand the horse upright, or colour it white? I *feel* that I am... and without some delineation, some definition of what hoodening really is, the term itself becomes meaningless. A morris dancer with a wooden horse doth not a hoodener make. But they could equally say "Maylam's book never mentions hoodeners having a written script: your group are just revivalists who perverted the old ways".

Granted, the horseplay of our village team 100 years ago was very different from the play we write anew every year now. It was rougher then, for a start (in 1966 one of the previous members said "they're a better class of people now... more inhibited"). We've had to change with the times, but as with cell renewal, it's like-for-like replacement, rotation not revolution. We're careful to retain the essence. As one example, the songs they sang before were quite different – but they were pop songs, not 'traditional folk ballads', so we too look at the charts each year and choose something we think will work with the audience (although we do change the words).

Perhaps as a consequence, our tradition has now continued far longer unbroken than any other documented group: some of our team have been performing every winter for over fifty years. We have members claiming direct descent from hoodeners a hundred years ago, as well as second-generation members in the current team. Above all, we have the continuity of Dobbin himself. And my gut feeling is that we will still be here long after the current boom and revival teams have faded away.

How does Hoodening actually appear in my life nowadays?

Generally, our custom is dormant through nine months of the year. Around September, we wait for Sam to have his annual hoodening dream, then arrange to meet up in one of the village pubs and discuss basic arrangements: who will write the script, what recent topics could be covered, who will perform, what venues will have us, where any monies raised should go, what tunes could be reworked into our song.

The first draft normally appears a few weeks later – often just five or six pages, starting with comments on local weather and the agricultural situation, then introducing the main theme and maybe even who gets killed and how (and how they are resuscitated: these all change every year). The scriptwriter will have printed off copies, so we'll meet at Street Acre, read through silently, offer feedback, and discuss any updates on the overall situation. That's normally all – but even so, each meeting tends to last two hours. (Any longer than that and we'd suffocate… flatulence seems to be an integral part of any hoodeners' gathering!) We're not yet 'in character' – no method acting, thank you – but we do refer to each other by our hoodening names.

A few weeks later we'll probably have a second draft, up to ten pages, most of the storyline now in there but without 'the cause', i.e. the lines at the end mentioning the charity of the year, which is often decided last minute. We might try reading it out loud, but probably just once, all seated with coffee and our semi-traditional "hoodeners' biscuits". Some members other than the scriptwriter may have brought along a few lines of their own, or suggestions to how to improve the existing ones – there's a fine line between getting out the dreaded 'blue pencil' (once wielded by a scriptwriter's wife to deadly effect, to bowdlerize all of his funniest lines), and becoming too offensive or controversial for modern times.

From then on it tends to be a weekly meeting. The script changes every week – adding lines about the latest news, or removing references to 'old' news that happened a month ago and will have been forgotten by Christmas. Checking that our favourite words are in there (p'r'aps you need to be a hoodener to know why roundabouts get mentioned so often), working out what props are needed this year and how to make or source them cheaply. Sharing information on the latest village happenings… my wife calls that part gossiping, but it's an integral part of binding the team together, and ensuring what we do is relevant. Agreeing who will write any 'special lines' for particular venues. Reading through the script again, sometimes even twice in an evening.

All of a sudden, it's one week to go. "Here's the song, lads!" Run it through once. Run the script twice, the second time standing up to check positions for obvious problems. Everyone's still reading from the printout – nobody has learnt more than their own first two or three lines. Bolder ones may even suggest that certain lines don't sound right due to the pronunciation or emphasis. I persuade everyone to run the song again – they'll never learn it anyway, but it's worth a try. Posters have been printed, and the website is getting updated with the latest list of likely locations and dates/times.

First day, two hours before first performance. We're in costume, albeit not yet corked up. "Scripts down!" (which in practice means inside the hat, in the pocket, or behind the back). That command came from our prompter: she's basically in charge now, with good reason. The play should take around twenty minutes, but the first attempt takes around fifty, largely because we're getting so much wrong and falling about laughing. The three-minute song takes three, because one of the team can sing (accompanied by a monotone drone from the others). "Not too bad" we blithely say. "It was rubbish!" replies the prompter, "From the top, again!". Second run-through takes only forty minutes. "Again!" and we're down to around thirty. We're already late – it's a well-known fact that hoodeners are never on time – but we have got four places to get around tonight, so we burn the corks, grab the props and carol sheets, decide who's driving (gone are the days when we walked everywhere), water the garden, and set out. Dobbin's awake!

The first venue this year is a brewery some distance outside the village. They've decided to put us out on the forecourt instead of inside the chiller room – to be honest, it's hard to tell which would be colder. There's an audience of maybe thirty people, two or three familiar faces but most have never seen us, have no idea what we're about, and can't hear us anyway. Yet they laugh along with some of the jokes, laugh at other lines we didn't realize were funny, and throw a few coppers in the nosebag. After fifty minutes or so we share a welcome beer before weeing* away to the next venue (*technical term, clear to those who've been there).

Number two is a private party, just ten people in their living room. It's a warm reception – mid-script, Dobbin hurls in a howl about the heat of his hessian. They sing the carols well, but we only do a couple because there's a delicious spread of food awaiting us. On to number three, a pub who've booked us for three gigs. The landlord knows the drill – he listens keenly to the special lines, and even before we've finished the script, six beers await us to sip while we sing. If not, the carols would start with "The First No-Ale". The adrenaline and alcohol have kicked in now, so the play is down to twenty-five minutes – partly because we skipped a page. Over our second beer we have a debrief to work out what went wrong. Then it's another wee to signal the cars are leaving, and we soon arrive at the last one of the night, another pub, full of locals who get all the lines and dare to heckle. Another tradition: we each feel the weight of the nosebag and guess how much has been raised – we'll know in a day or two. Life is good.

Days two and three proceed in similar vein. Gradually we remember more words, and hone our timings – although we forget everything if there's a Sunday in between. We keep an eye out for our groupies: a bunch of blokes who rent a minibus to come and view us at a different hostelry every year. We meet old friends, including retired members who make perspicacious remarks about the script and song. Some people say they've already seen us twice this year – "that means you'll know more of the script than we do!". And so we arrive at the final day, 23 December. For tradition, we start at Street Acre – Dobbin urges us to get through the script quickly so he can wolf down some bean stew. On then to the last two venues, generally on foot as we try to keep the final day all within the village. The words are now flowing, even the song's quite good, and at the final performance, I traditionally do every carol on the sheet, with a mad dash at the end of Twelve Days (followed by a pint in one).

We sign the prompter's script, and most of us then stay for a few more hours, setting the world to rights, but also making suggestions for next year. It's generally agreed that on Boxing Day we'll walk over the marshes to Boyden Gate to watch the mummers and morris, where we'll also hear how much we raised. And then that's it – or almost.

For me, each year finishes when I rest Dobbin on my shoulder and walk home. It's the middle of the night, the village is dark and silent, except for his bells. I walk in the middle of the road, because this is *our* village. Dobbin – and in a sense, George too – has been here for centuries, and if a car were to come, they'd just have to wait. It's a magical feeling, impossible to put into words. But once I'm home and Dobbin is back in his stable – until his rebirth in nine months' time – the most important season of the year, the climax of months of preparation, is complete. Nothing comparable could follow that. The rest is silence.

APPENDIX 1:
MODERN HOODENING VERSES

'The Hooden Horse' by Phil Martin

Recorded by Drohne on the album *We Bring You a King with a Head of Gold* (2011).

> Please welcome in the hooden horse, for he is a jovial beast
> Jangling bell, beady eye, clacking of nailed jaw
> So give a welcome, give a cheer to bless you for the coming year
> When winter time is round again, the hooden horse is here
>
> Please welcome in the hooden horse, he's as black as Old Nick's beard
> Come to mourn the passing darkness of the year
> Give a welcome, give a fee, touch his forelock, you'll not need
> If winter time is round again, the hooden horse is here
>
> Please welcome in the hooden horse, for he's a tired old beast
> Drovers worked him hard for 12 month of the year
> Bring his wages, bring his pay, he's come to sweep this year away
> If winter time is round again, the hooden horse is here
>
> Please welcome in the hooden horse, he's the beast to lift the curse
> Of long dark nights that chill our bones, pastures and our homes
> Bring some cheese, bring some bread, give a cheer to raise the dead
> If winter time is round again, the hooden horse is here
> Bring some cheese, bring some bread, give a cheer to raise the dead
> If winter time is round again, the hooden horse is here

'The Finest Hooden Horse' by Gail Duff (1998)

Written for the first Hoodening Moot in 1998, which was held at the Chequers, Doddington as a charity event, organized by Phil Bleazey.

> We have come up to Doddington all on a midwinter's day,
> And brought the finest Hooden Horse that ever was fed on hay.
>
> Chorus: O it's the truth, the truth indeed, sir, the truth it is I say.
> He is the finest Hooden Horse that ever was fed on hay.
>
> Now this horse is very handsome, you never would call him poor
> He'll have you all for dinner, sir, and still he'll ask for more.

Now his head is made of wood, sir, cut from the walnut tree,
The finest piece of wood, sir, that ever you did see.

Now this horse he has some eyes, sir, that shine out in the dark
They shine like the Devil himself, sir, and cause the dogs to bark.

Once the teeth upon this horse, sir, were big as standing stones
But now they've worn away, sir, from grinding up the bones.

This horse has got a throat, sir, as deep as any well,
If you should fall inside, sir, you'd fall right down to hell.

The mane upon this horse, sir, is very long and coarse,
And if you try to grab it, sir, it'll rip you like the gorse.

The back upon this horse, sir, is very strong and wide,
It'll seat a hundred men, sir, and away with them he'll ride.

His hooves are round and iron-shod and make the sparks to fly,
But don't you stand too close, sir, or he'll kick you in the eye.

He'll lash his tail around, sir, and crack it like a whip,
And if you get too close, sir, you're sure to feel the tip.

So now you've met our horse, sir, we think you will agree,
A meaner looking horse, sir, never walked so free.

'The Hooden Horse' by Gail Duff (11 November 2003)

Way back in about 1970, a member of a Kent morris side, who shall be nameless, told me that 'Hooden' came from 'Odin', probably fanciful but a good story. Then I got to thinking about the white stallions that the Saxons kept for seven years as leaders of a sacred herd and then sacrificed. Needing a new song for yet another Hoodening Moot, I returned to the theme over thirty years later. Thanet was, after all, the first Saxon territory. Whether you believe it or not, it made a good song, and a good play.

> Old Horse, Old Horse, what brought you here,
> Linked with the land more than two thousand year,
> Leading us in the ancient rhyme
> And bringing cheer at winter time?
>
> Leader of the herd was I.
> Over the Island my hooves did fly,
> White as the driven winter's snow,
> The land was blessed where I did go.

I ruled seven years by Odin's grace,
Then one more grew to take my place.
At Yule came the flash of the sacred knife.
For the sake of the land I gave my life.

Into the earth my blood did flow,
For the trees to fruit and the corn to grow.
They drank to me as the Yule log burned,
That they might thrive when the year did turn.

Then came a man with a silver cross,
Preaching sin. It was all our loss.
They whipped me, stripped me and buried me deep,
And left me there in the earth to sleep.

But I am the soul of this land by the sea,
And I am a part of its memory.
I haunted the coast on a Midwinter night,
And put the Church into a fright.

When starving workers knelt down and prayed,
I was the one who came to their aid.
I gave my spirit to a skull with a hood,
And they carried me round for the people's good.

Now my head is wood and my eyes are glass,
I clack my jaw as you go past.
I caper and prance in the Midwinter game,
But still I carry Odin's name.

So in comes the Horse and all his men,
He's come to see you once again.
The Hooden Horse of Odin's line,
To bring us a blessed winter time.

'The Wagoner's Tale' by Gail Duff (2017)

Dedicated to my great grandfather, Joseph Cheshire, who was a real head wagoner at Stoke Farm, Stoke Mandeville, Aylesbury, Bucks, around the beginning of the 20th century. Being a Hoodening Wagoner gives me a sense of continuity. I wrote this to sing at the launch of George Frampton's book, *Discordant Comicals* (2018).

> When first I went a-Hoodening, a-Hoodening did go,
> I thought we'd end up in the ditch in sorrow, grief and woe,
> But many were the good times that we did undergo.

Chorus:
Sing woa, me lads, drive, on, me lads
Drive on, me lads, drive on.
There's none can drive the Hooden Horse like Joe the Wagoner.

My name is Joe the Carter, a wagoning man am I,
In charge of all the wagons and the farmer's men beside,
And one year in November, they took me for a ride.

Well, Christmas time is coming, Boss, and we're all short of pay,
And, since you are the Gaffer, we've got something to say,
Why don't we go Hoodening, to drive our cares away?

Now Dick can be the Rider, and Tom can be the fool,
And Harry there, he's just a lad, we'll dress him like a girl,
He'll sweep the ground before us and put folks in a whirl.

We've dug up old dead Dobbin's skull and stuck it on a pole,
And found a bit of sacking that isn't full of holes,
We'll put it on young Jimmy, with his face blacked up with coal.

I've found me concertina and I can play you round,
We'll have a big collecting box for pennies and for pounds,
We'll do a bit of capering and acting like a clown.

Now, Carter Joe, there's one more man to make our team complete,
You must be the Wagoner, all dressed up smart and neat,
You'll lead us round the houses and up the village street.

Now Christmas time is come, me lads, what pleasures shall we see,
We'll count up our collection and spend our money free,
And we will raise our glasses to our jovial company.

'Being Horse' by Sonia Overall (2019)

This poem was composed for the short film Being Horse (2019) created collaboratively by James Frost and Sonia Overall, and screened in the exhibition. The film was shot from a camera mounted inside Jim 'the Ram' Bywater's May Day Horse while it walked the procession at Whitstable.

> Are you ready?
> The one within sees through a veil: dust and cloth, a column of wood. Blurs and bursts of light. A chequerboard of seeing. Hessian presses close, obscuring forms and distances. But my glass eye takes you in.

You look at me and see the hinge and snap. I am a swaying pillar of sackcloth moving in steady time. I am coming towards you. I am immoveable. I go where I will.
My flanks are creased. My mane is a tangle of yarn. Hawthorn blossom hangs, flesh-and-honey sweet, at my leather ears.
I taste the rust of the sea between hobnail teeth.

The harbour wall. The one within cannot see its feet: tread carefully. Its arms grow numb with weight and lack of use. Sweat gathers in its hairline.
The ground moves, narrows to a point. A top-heavy, bipedal balancing act. All feeling is there, in the soles.

Precipice and pebble.
Oyster shells sharp-edged, waiting in their unmade beds of grit and silt.
Broken bottles. The stinging ring-pulls of cans. Picnic debris, the detritus of passers-by.
Flotsam, jetsam. Fibres of transit.

I rise above, aloft: a pedestal.

Listen. Do you hear the waves against the drum? Do you hear the gulls against the tread and skip?

I am coming. Watch me, the prow of a ship, pressing a path.
The wet-iron stink of crabstick and whelk. The blue-and-gold borders of fish market. The seaside familiars.

I am aloof. I am a stalker. I am the stealer of ice-creams, the terror of babes, the rousing roister-doister of dog-walkers. The bane of bus drivers. I preen. I pose. I pounce.

You may not look at me now, but you feel me here. I am impossible. You refuse me, turn away. But you will not forget me.
I am the mote in the eye, the unfeasible at the edges, unfathomable.
Pretend you cannot see me if you must. I see you. We see you. We are relentless.

Are you ready?

APPENDIX 2: MODERN HOODENING PLAYS

St Nicholas-at-Wade with Sarre 1966 play
© The Hoodeners

MOLLY:
> The Hoodeners are 'ere!
> Make way for the Hoodeners!
> All right Joe, they're all ready for us

JOE:
> Now then, mind you behave yerself,
> Remember where we are.

ADAM:
> No knocking the furniture over, it's Mr Cole's house

MOLLY:
> Don't mess up the carpets like yer did at the vicarage

COLIN:
> 'e won't budge!

JOE:
> Dig yer 'eels in boy!
> Woah! Woah!
> Steady boy, steady!
> There now, quiet as a mouse,
> He knows he's in ol' Will Cole's house

COLIN:
> Fine oats and nice fresh grass

JOE:
> Ouch! He's bin and bit my...

MOLLY:
> Remember where you are Joe

ADAM:
> Ouch! He's bin and bit my shin

MOLLY:
> Hold on boy! Hold on...

JOE:
> Sit down lad

MOLLY:
> He's thrown the boy
> Lift his head, pat his cheeks
> There's some life there if he squeaks

JOE:
> Not a murmur, not a wink
> Dead as mutton, now I think
> Great big bruise all black and yeller

ADAM:
> He's been and killed the poor young feller

JOE:
> A dent an inch deep in his roof
> Made by cruel ol' Dobbin's hoof

ADAM:
> Tell his mother her boy's no more
> Nothing can the lad restore

MOLLY:
> Put two pennies on his eyes
> Like they do when someone dies (sob, sob)

ADAM:
> Use 'is scarf to tie 'is jaw
> He won't be wanting it no more

MOLLY:
> Good-bye to his Mum, and love 'im

JOE:
> Soon the daisies he'll be shovin'
> Roots of dandelion be eatin'

MOLLY:
> Wrap 'im up in pure white sheeting
> Make his shrouds of finest linen
> Lord forgive the poor lad's sinning

JOE:
> Amen (quietly)

MOLLY:
> A carpenter for old Will Cole
> Perhaps he'll bury the poor young soul

JOE:
> In the cold ground, he'll abide

Study joinery from inside
ALL:
Study joinery from inside

[They all lift him up and wrap the boy in a sheet]

MOLLY:
Tell the parson, fetch the choir
ADAM:
The finest Daimler we will hire
MOLLY:
Plant Colin Bean in Shuart Lane
JOE:
Never to sprout up again
ALL:
Never to sprout up again

[Weeping, wailing and gnashing of teeth, with the funeral march]

ADAM:
He moved!
MOLLY:
He moved!
JOE:
Give 'im something to drink
ADAM:
Can you hear me Colin lad?
COLIN:
Where am I — is that you Joe?
MOLLY:
How you feeling Boy?
JOE:
Lift 'im up
ADAM:
Steady does it Boy
MOLLY:
How you feeling?

COLIN:
> Right as rain
> Ready to start off again
> But first let's pay old Dobbin back
> For giving my head such a crack

JOE:
> Ah! and I'm going to beat 'is hide
> For lacerating my backside

ADAM:
> Ah! and I'm going to do 'im in
> For nearly breaking my poor shin

[All beat the living daylights out of Dobbin!]

JOE:
> Tell Colin you're sorry
> Ah, there now

ALL:
> Boy and horse are friends once more
> Head and eyes no longer sore
> Dobbin now is all submission
> Having learned his hardest lesson
> Half starved he is now, poor nag
> Something please to fill his bag
> Do not burst out the door
> Give us something, good friends, for...
> If ye the Hooden horse do feed
> Throughout the year ye shall not need.

Whitstable Hoodening Play

Characters:-
1 Molly – dresses in skirt & apron, shawl or cloak, bonnet or headscarf but is not a drag part, simply a man wearing a primitive disguise. Carries a besom broom.
2 Hooden Horse – head is carved of wood, on a short wooden pole. Lower Jaw is hinged and operated with a length of cord. A horse cloth of brown hessian or black material is attached to the head & covers the Hoodener to about knee-length.
3 Wagoner – top hat, tail coat, neckerchief, white shirt, coloured waistcoat, breeches or trousers tied at knee with twine. Carries a whip and leads the Horse with the bridle.
4 Rider – as Wagoner, without top hat, tail coat & whip. Wears flat cap or bowler instead. May carry a hand bell.
5 Fool – optional part. Dresses as Wagoner & Rider, but shabby, with tatters or patchwork. May carry a hand bell.
6 Musicians/Singers – as many as you like, male or female, dress in character if possible.
Molly enters first & clears an area with broom. Other Hoodeners follow, when in position they sing the Blean or Whitstable Hoodening Song.

> The Whitstable Hoodeners Song
>
> First the Molly Man comes in
> That's turned his cloak all outsides-in
> He can't be seen by devil or man
> So drives Old Nick from the door
>
> Comes the turning of the year
> All good men have duty clear
> To bring good luck on the winter drear
> And ride the Hooden Horse
>
> In comes the Hooden Horse at his ease
> As kind a nag as takes the breeze
> But anyone here should him displease
> He'll kick you back to the door
>
> Next the Wagoner's come to the chase
> With whip and halter to settle the case
> He'll Hoodener bridle with leather trace
> And lead him back to the door

The Rider he's a brisk young blood
He'll Hoodener straddle and ride to the wood
He don't think much of the sticks and mud
When he stumbles back to the door

And when that we have done the task
And Hooden-Horse is ridden at last
We'll sing good cheer and raise a glass
And dance auay from your door

Blean Song

Three jolly Hoodening Boys
Lately come from Town
Apples or for money
We search the country round
What you please to give us
Happy we shall be
God bless every poor man
Who's got an apple tree
Hats full, caps full
Half bushel bags full
God bless every poor man
Who's got an apple tree

Team enter in order (Molly, Wagoner leading Horse, Rider, Fool)
All sing Blean Hoodening Song

WAGONER
> In comes Horse and all his men
> He's come to see you once again

MOLLY
> When was the last time?

WAGONER
> I don't know!
> He has travelled through both frost and snow.
> He has travelled far and near,
> from over there to right by here.

Now to the [insert pub name here] he will go!
MOLLY
And when will he be back?
WAGONER
I don't know!
And who are you to ask me so?
MOLLY
They calls me Molly though my name be Polly
And I say all this will end in folly!
WAGONER
How say you so?
MOLLY
I don't know
– but what I say is always so!
WAGONER
Horse – there's a fool there

(Horse attacks Molly – Molly beats off with broom)

MOLLY
That's an evil looking horse
WAGONER
What did you say? That was ill-meant
There's no finer horse in the whole of Kent!
MOLLY
I've seen a finer horse than that, while travelling the county round,
Its girth was nothing half so fat, and all four hooves and legs were sound
WAGONER
Where did you see this horse?
MOLLY
Down Bogshole Lane beneath the drain
WAGONER
That was a Dead Horse! What use is a Dead Horse? What can he do?
MOLLY
Everything that he can, and without biting you
- and it was better looking too!

(Horse very sad)

WAGONER
> That was a nasty thing to say
> – you've quite upset our horse today.
> What reason was it brought you here
> to make our horse so sad and queer?

MOLLY
> The reason why I do not know,
> but before I am not here I will go.
> I'll come when I am here of course
> – but tell us further of this horse.

WAGONER
> Why this horse has a back like a beam
> A belly like a bream
> A neck like a drake
> A head like a snake
> A foot like a cat
> And a tail like a rat
> And like the wind he'll go!

(All make farting noises. Horse runs off.)

MOLLY
> Ay Ay (laughing) but bid him whoa!

(Horse doesn't stop until Wagoner uses "hay" instead of "whoa")

WAGONER
> It's the sight of your face makes him frightened and riot,
> He just needs a rider to keep him happy and quiet.
> Hoy hoy – come here boy (to Rider)

RIDER
> In comes I, I don't know why

WAGONER
> Why – to ride the horse of course!

RIDER
> I'm not riding him – he's far too grim

WAGONER
> He won't hurt you or kill you dead
> He won't harm one hair of your head

RIDER
Won't he?
MOLLY
No – he don't like the hairs – he spits them out afterwards!
WAGONER

(grabbing Rider by back of belt)

You'll ride that horse, your duty calls,
'cos if you don't, you'll lose your...
MOLLY
Hey – it's a family show!
RIDER
I think it hard but I will do it
though I fear I'll maybe rue it.

(Rider jumps on horse, and rides for a bit. Horse throws rider to the ground where he lays motionless)

MOLLY
Your rider has fallen on his head
– I fear he may be slightly dead.
It's as I said would come to pass...
WAGONER
Why don't you stick it up your...?
MOLLY
Oy! I've told you about that before.
He's not dead quite,
I'll see if I can put him right

(Jabs rider with broom. Rider sits up)

RIDER
I'll not be doing that again
– I might have shaken loose my brain
WAGONER
You wouldn't miss it!
Enough of this joking
– this horse must be broken

RIDER

You won't get me again to try
– you'll need a bigger fool than I

WAGONER

If this is so – what shall we do?
There is no bigger fool than you!

RIDER

Oh yes there is

MOLLY

Oh no there isn't!

(Fool is strolling around in front of the audience. Oh yes there…/oh no goes on a bit)

WAGONER

How so then?

(Molly points at Fool. Fool is unaware of this. Wagoner creeps up and taps Fool on the shoulder.)

WAGONER

Come sir, and take our Rider's place,
we trust that you will not disgrace.
Though I must ask how are you known?

MOLLY

He's got to carve it on the stone

FOOL

How I'm known is plain to see,
I'd be a fool to hark to thee.

WAGONER

Can you ride though?

FOOL

With saddle and bridle I can rid-le

WAGONER

What can you ride?

FOOL

I can ride anything!

WAGONER

Can you ride this horse?

FOOL
>That's not anything!

WAGONER
>Now don't upset the horse again,
>he's already broke his rein.
>You'll upset him sure as eggs,
>because he's only got two legs

FOOL
>Oh no he hasn't (oh yes he has)

WAGONER
>How so then?

FOOL
>Are his legs on his back or his front?

WAGONER
>Front

FOOL
>So they can't be his hind legs

WAGONER
>No?

FOOL
>So they must be his 1-2-3-fore legs

Molly & Wagoner give vent to natural reaction. Fool skips out.

WAGONER
>Enough of your joking
>this horse needs to be broken

(Improvise search, getting volunteer from the crowd. A small child is ideal. Horse submits tamely).

WAGONER
>Ladies and Gentlemen, one and all
>Our rider is mended, our hoodening's ended
>We trust that we have not offended

MOLLY
>What we beg is but small
>But is obliged to serve us all

WAGONER
>So pass the hat, ladies and gentlemen please
>For they're tidy down the High Street

MOLLY
>They're middling down the Wall

WAGONER
>But as for the Island wallahs

BOTH
>The buggers won't pay at all

Finish with Blean Hoodening Song

Tonbridge Hooden Horse Play

Written by Geoff Doel & Nick Miller, 1979, incorporating elements from other British horse plays.

Characters: Wagoner, Horse, Rider, Molly (man/woman with broom), Doctor, Musician/Singer
(Old Horse song & Molly sweeps the stage with broom. Enter Wagoner & Horse dropping turds)

>Old horse old horse what brought you here
>Carted stones this many's the year
>Killed by stones and sore abuse
>They salt you down for sailors' use
>A warrior am I and at war I've been
>Fighting for my country and king
>Now I'm old and I'm in decay
>It's poor old horse get on your way
>My keeping once was the stable wall
>Free from all cold winds and harm
>Now in the fields I am forced to go
>Turned out in the cold and rain and snow
>My feeding once was the oats and hay
>That grew in the fields and the meadows gay
>Now I'll get no such at all
>But pull at the short grass by the wall

WAGONER
>Now ladies and gentlemen just look around.
>Did you ever see a better class of beast out of England's ground?
>He's an eye like a hawk, a neck like a swan,
>A pair of ears cut from a leather apron.
>When he opens his mouth his head comes loose,
>If you look down his throat you can see holes on his shoes. (Horse stamps)
>Whoa, stand still!
>He's a very fine horse, he's very fine bred (Horse turns)
>On Tonbridge oats this horse has been fed. (Horse drops another turd)
>He's won the Derby and the Oaks,
>And finished up pulling an old milk float.
>So stand round Dobbin and show yourself. (Horse turns again to audience)

RIDER (ENTERS, LOOKS AT HORSE CRITICALLY)

Wherever did you get that old bag of bones? (Horse glares at rider)

WAGONER

From... (some local place rhyming with a Christian name – e.g. 'from Thanet, Janet')

RIDER

How much did you give for him?

WAGONER

... (comic response citing some current worthless or ludicrous item)

RIDER

I wouldn't give a penny for him.

WAGONER

He's got more spirit than you can tame; I bet you couldn't ride him.

RIDER

Nothing easier, poor old nag!

(RIDER mounts horse, who cavorts and throws him. MOLLY gloats over fallen RIDER, who gets up, seizes broom from MOLLY and knocks the horse on the head, who 'dies')

WAGONER

Why you young ruffian, you've killed my poor old horse.
Now what can we do?
Is there a horse doctor to be found,
Able to raise this dead horse from the ground?

DOCTOR

I am a Doctor from the NHS – the National Horse Service. I have aids to cure all equine ills. Harnessing my skills for the good of the community. Famed for my unbridled wit. The main Doctor... (ALL cough) Why, whatever's the matter with this poor old nag?

WAGONER

We were hoping you could tell us that.

DOCTOR

I give no opinion without a fee.

WAGONER

What is your fee Mr Noble Doctor?

DOCTOR

A pint of beer for the diagnosis and a glass of whisky for the cure.

WAGONER
>Done

DOCTOR
>(aside) You have been!
>(publicly) Very well. First for my diagnosis.

(DOCTOR examines the horse. He pretends to cut the horse open and extracts the 'guts', which he invites the audience to examine)

DOCTOR
>Nothing wrong with those (throwing the guts into the audience)
>It is my considered opinion, having examined the corporate parts of this inanimate quadruped... (he is interrupted by the WAGONER and together they count the horse's legs) ... this inanimate tripod, that this horse is dead.

WAGONER
>But what about the cure?

DOCTOR
>It is not a mere blow
>That has laid this creature low,
>And no remedy can I produce
>To reign in and harness his spirit loose,
>Without the aid of a maiden's kiss
>To raise this horse to life and bliss.

DOCTOR, WAGONER & RIDER (TOGETHER)
>Is there a maiden to be found,
>Able to raise this dead horse from the ground?

WAGONER
>Molly, find a maiden

(MOLLY selects a maiden from the audience and asks her to kiss the horse, recommending the head)

DOCTOR
>Life now returns and through these limbs doth flow,
>Revealing more than you may wish to know.

WAGONER
>Thank you noble Doctor and young maiden
>Who'd have imagined that from the dead this horse would be raise'n?
>Now my horse is a magic horse, as I will demonstrate.

(asks comic questions as appropriate) e.g.

> Give me a number between 1 and 500
> Show me the lady who threw the bedclothes off last night dreaming of her sweetheart
> Show me the sweetheart she threw the bedclothes off
> Show me the person who understood every word of this play...can you explain it to us!
> Show me the patron of the arts who's going to buy the Tonbridge Mummers a round of drinks.
> Now, from the light into the dark, show me the biggest rogue here.
> (HORSE roams around the audience and eventually selects the WAGONER whom he drives off stage to MUSIC)

Swale Hoodening Play

Synopsis

Wagoner and Horse meet Molly. Discourse on Molly being Devil watcher, and Horse being good luck. Rider dared to ride horse. Swears by devil that he will. Falls off (caused by devil). Molly picks him up. Wagoner looks for some one else to ride the Horse. Spies Fool / Devil (Molly sees him not as he is tending to Rider) Wagoner asks Fool to ride. Horse hides from him. Fool / Devil won't ride but wants to take the Rider away. Molly looks up at commotion. Sees Fool / Devil as what he is. Talks with him before putting him out with broom. Wagoner says Horse must still be ridden. Gets volunteer from audience. Molly does epilogue.

Team enter in order (Molly, Wagoner leading Horse, Rider, Fool/Devil)

WAGONER
>Winter comes – the sky is dark
>The trees reduced to leafless bark
>But through the snow with measured tread
>Now comes the Horse with hooded head
>To bring you laughter, luck, and cheer
>To light the turning of the year.
>So welcome Horse and let him play
>And his luck with you this night will stay.
>'tis strange thing, Horse, that here do stand
>with woman's clothes and yet man's hand
>Methinks we ought to ask her grace
>whyfore her clothes don't match her face?

MOLLY
>O ask, for 'tis my ancient duty
>To dress so fine in all my beauty
>For to trap the devil so
>Who is deceived by woman's show
>Then shall I banish him the room
>With this my weapon – trusty broom

WAGONER
>Deceived by you? That would be weird
>Methinks you should not show your beard
>I cannot think Old Nick so stupid
>That for your face he'd pray to Cupid!

MOLLY
    Ay – you are right there, as a rule
    But sometimes Nick will play the fool
    And so I'll wait… To pass the time
    Tell me of your Horse so fine

WAGONER
    This Horse?
    Why 'tis older than England, older than thou,
    'twas thought a God, but is mortal now
    So long we keep old Horse alive
    Shall Kent be garden of this land
    And Men of Kent o'er all shall stand
    This Horse is a marvel without peer
    With fiery eye and upright ear
    With legs of iron and hooves of steel
    and fiery breath that soon you'll feel…
    He needs to be ridden, that calms him down
    And he'll walk sweetly round the town…
    There's a lad down there will fit the part
    Though perhaps he doesn't have the heart

(pointing to Rider)

RIDER
    Not have the heart! How say you that?
    For I have ridden on the flat,
    And jumps a'many I have dared
    And never yet have I been scared
    To ride a nag eighteen hands high
    He don't scare me…

WAGONER
    He will, by and by!

WAGONER
    Go tender boy, you need not ride
    'tis vanity all and youthful pride
    You cannot ride old Horse I say
    You're much too young – go on your way.

RIDER
    I'll ride him I swear, by all in Hell

And still I swear I'll ride him well
If by this Horse should I be thrown
May the Devil take me for his own!

(Molly looks up at this. Rider mounts Horse and rides him, quite well, until Horse is spooked by Fool / Devil, and Rider falls off, appearing stunned or dead).

WAGONER
The rider's thrown and lies full still
Horse – you didn't need to kill.
MOLLY (GOES TO RIDER)
The boy's not dead – his body's hale
But I fear me that his soul doth fail
'tis never wise the devil to call
For then bad chance is sure to fall.

(Feels Rider's pulse and lays him back on the ground. Doesn't look at action, or notice Fool / Devil).

WAGONER
(to Fool / Devil) Sir – come and ride the horse for us
As you're the cause of all this fuss
You must for it was sight of thee
Led Horse to cause this misery.
FOOL
When I have what's mine then I'll be gone
I'm no rider for your fun
WAGONER
(Aside) Where's sense in that? This man's a fool
And I'd not use him as a rule…
But riders here are looking scarce
With one laid ready on the hearse.
(To Devil) You caused the fall – Now make it right
And ride the Horse for us tonight.

(Molly has looked up, and followed this conversation. He can see, though Wagoner cannot, that the Fool is really the Devil, summoned by the Rider's oath)

FOOL

    Nay I'll not ride, to bring you luck in house and hearth, hereafter
    I have a better end than that that's bound to bring no laughter
    For stay, here is a friend of mine *(pointing at Rider)* who's called on me in ire
    Needs must I take him home with me to warm him by **my** fire.

MOLLY

    You think to fool us all too quick
    And make off with your prize
    But I know you true to be Old Nick
    And Horse sees your disguise.
    It's true the boy did loudly call
    And on your Grace did swear
    But he's no soul for Hell so foul
    You shall not take him there

(Fool / Devil thinks that Molly is a woman)

FOOL

    Come on good dame, 'twould be a shame
    If thou went as well as he
    For hell is hot, so vex me not
    Lest I grant thee misery
    For I am the Devil as you've said
    And safe from woman's tears
    And Horse and Wagoner full are stayed

(Devil points hand at Wagoner and Horse, who both freeze in place)

    I've caught them unawares.
    So lest thee with the devil sleep
    And feel a different kind of **heat**
    I say run off – on dainty feet
    Or the boy's own fate you'll share!

(Devil has come up to Molly, and is in range of Molly's suppressed violence).

MOLLY

    Oh Devil who in Hell hath ruled
    How could you be so lightly fooled

> I am no woman for you to taunt
> No damsel shy or maiden aunt
> For I am devil-hater full
> Who will not suffer you at all
> But bids thee gone and straight to Hell
> In whose mystery fires you dwell
> By my broom of magic made
> Of oak and ash and thorn
> I bid thee go into the shade
> And leave all here alone!

(Molly is bashing Fool /Devil with broom)

> Go you will, though man you spelled
> As he was unprepared
> Horse himself will see you off
> He's not so easy snared

(Devil has now come in reach of Horse, who has been faking it. Horse attacks Devil as well)

DEVIL
> I am beset and cannot stay
> You've won the round I see
> Your Horse has routed Devil
> and he can do naught but flee.
> The boy is safe, his soul is yours
> But for a little time
> For if he do not rein his tongue
> He will again be mine!

(Devil leaves. Rider wakes up. Wagoner is released from stasis)

WAGONER
> I see I was not right to scoff
> Not fair to make you rise
> For the Devil you've seen off
> By guile and by disguise.
> And though Horse here has proved his worth

>   Yet still is he un-ridden
>   And lest the Devil should return
>   A Rider now is bidden

RIDER

>   I had my chance and fared it hard
>   I will not chance again
>   But surely one from out the crowd
>   Will ride him on the rein?

WAGONER

>   Come sirs and maids
>   And ride the Horse
>   He can but bring you luck
>   And with the Devil safely gone
>   There is no chance he'll buck.
>   *(or)* There's none will give a... *bugger*

(Volunteer from the audience rides the Horse. All clap him/her. Horse is docile)

MOLLY

>   And now our play is at an end
>   And Horse has been full ridden
>   The Rider's well, and safe from Hell
>   Where the Devil now is hidden.
>   The Wagoner's learnt his words to mind
>   And give to all fair greeting
>   Molly's turned his cloak about
>   And give old Nick a beating.
>   If you have enjoyed at all
>   The measure of these verses
>   We hope that pleased, you one and all
>   Will thank us from your purses!

The Canterbury Hooden Horse

Sonia Overall, November 2018

Cast: Musician, Molly, Rider, Wagoner
Enter All: Musician plays tune, Molly sweeps, Wagoner leads in Horse

Wagoner
    Behold, one and all, this steed so fine!
    This noble specimen equine!
    His hooves are sturdy as founding stones   (Horse stamps)
    His back is broad as a barrel vault   (Horse arches back)
    His ears are eager as flying buttresses   (Horse wags head)
    And his teeth are a chorus of choirboys.   (Horse snaps teeth)

Rider
    What's this lumpy old sack?

Wagoner
    How dare you insult my horse's pride?

Rider
    I could get onto his back.

Wagoner
    He's a finer beast than you could ride!

Rider attempts three times to mount Horse, then kicks and 'kills' it.

Wagoner
    My horse is low and lies so still –
    Good thing I have a doctor's skill!
    Through the chancel and into the vestry

(Wagoner cuts into horse, pulls out guts)

    Aha! A surplus of surplices!

(Wagoner throws guts)

    Now I have removed all this
    We just require a maiden's kiss –

WAGONER & RIDER
>Is there a maiden to be found,
>To raise this dead horse from the ground?
>Molly, find a maiden!

MOLLY selects a maiden from the audience and asks her to kiss the horse. HORSE revives. WAGONER listens to HORSE's chest.

WAGONER
>His lungs are lusty as organ bellows
>His veins and arteries the pipes and stops   (HORSE drops turds)
>And the valves appear to be working!

HORSE drops several turds. MUSICIAN plays. Exeunt all, chasing HORSE, MOLLY sweeping and cursing.

The Hoodening Play of Dover Tales

Nic Lucas, 2016

MOLLY [WITH BESSOM]
    Step aside, Step aside and give me way,
    I sweep the ground this hoodening day
    I am come from Dover Tone
    where as Molly Long legs I am known.
    My little sister you may have noun…
    Molly No-Legs of great renown…
    No-Legs… it was often said,
    'cos she was allus found in bed…
    and then if not in the sack…
    all could find her on her back.
    A woman of the oldest trade…
    she'd turn a trick for sailors quick, her money to be made.
    As for me I sweep the ground here all around,
    to make the way for our Hooden Horseplay
    it's here for Tom, Dick and Harry…
    so come in Joey do not tarry.

JOEY
    Step aside, Step aside and give room,
    In comes sailor Joey…. the horse's groom…
    In most my trades I am well versed,
    as Farrier and Ostler I comes in first…
    but as rider and jockey 'tis disgrace,
    'cos I allus ends up on my face .
    Now our horse is the finest to be seen,
    for he is HIPPO MARES the 'orse from the sea,
    descended for the steeds and bold deeds of Hengist and Horsa
    our Saxon forebears of years beforah.
    His name is ALBINUS INVICTUS for he is white and unbeaten
    as the old Dover cliffs and the chalk lying here beneath,
    but in order to make this all sound silly…
    DOBBIN is what we will call this filly
    I have his halter in my hand, to bring him in so he can stand.
    So ready now to heave mi Johnnies,
    with a heave'e, haul'e, altogether, steady we go… not hell for leather…

come now Molly give us a tug, so we can see his ugly mug

Rope hauling routine after a deal of to-ing and fro-ing

"I know this ain't a cow but let's see if we can milk it"
"this could be money for old rope" (etc. ad lib)

After a fair bit of shtick the mayor gets pulled in

MR MAYOR

Step aside, Step aside and make it thorough,
for I am the mayor of this here borough
mi name is Chump but call me Herbert,
cos I am famous for the fizzy sherbet.
As wagoner I own this 'orse
and we will bring him here in course,
but first we will with Hooden song regale you.

The Blean Song

One Two Three! Jolly Hoodening boys lately come to town
For apples and for money we search the county round
If you have no money happy we will be
God bless every poor man that's got an apple tree
Hats full, caps full, half a bushel bag full
God bless every poor man that's got an apple tree.

MAYOR

So Step aside all, Step aside, for in now comes our horse
The finest you will ever see so let him run this course.

Horse bursts / cavorting in, Joey grabs his rein, and horse and Joey dash around the place until they come to a halt, after a good few upsets and encounters with the crowd.

MOLLY

Call that a horse? I have seen better horse flesh on Frankie Di Tori's whip.
The poor little thing is so mangy and thin
is naught but an skelington covered in skin. *[sung]*
Send for the nacker Henry Pugh...
he'll turn old Dobbin into... strong glue.

MAYOR

    Mother Molly you are too cruel,
    this horse has a memory that will not forget
    your mean words that cause upset.
    Look he has the eye of a snake, the head of a hake,
    a neck like a spar and a back like a bar!
    What's more just fancy that he has 6 legs, and a tail like a rat!

JOEY

    A tail of a rat I plainly see
    but six legs please explain to me!

MAYOR

    We will count so you can see,
    call the numbers after me

Dobbin alternately lifts feet, the mayor counts, the cast repeats

    One – one, Two – two, Three –three
    Four – four, Five –five, Six –six

MOLLY

    Now that is strange and queer to me
    you count 6 but I saw 3?

MAYOR

    Ah not a diddle or a fiddle
    you saw the one that hung down in the middle…

[points at his own member]

    But let me explain it works like this… in the front there are two legs, they
    are his forelegs, so two legs and forelegs make six legs, so there,
    even a fool such as thee
    can work it out as plain to see.
    We must not wait or further blunder
    this horse must be broken, but not asunder
    So come on Joey do not stray,
    bound up on Dobbin without delay.
    Put him through his paces quick
    and have him leap my walking stick.
    He must be broke, or I will be…
    my shirt is on him at Aintree

> So come on Joey I'll count to three
> then on his back you must be.

[then proceeds counting up to three with several abortive attempt at mounting, ad libs etc. such as counting 1, 1½, 2, 2½, shouts like "blindfold him... no, you fool, the horse not the rider!" – when the rider finally gets on the horse it collapses... throwing Joey to floor... both dead...]

MAYOR
> Oh my lord what have you done?
> You've killed the 'orse so I'm undone

MOLLY
> And look my boy has come unstuck,
> so sod your 'orse an' champ his barley,
> let's us send for Captain Charley

Song Poor Old Man

> A poor old man came a-riding by,
> And we say so! And we hope so
> Says I, "Old man, your horse will die".
> Oh, poor old horse!
>
> And if he dies we'll tan his hide,
> And we say so! And we hope so
> But if he lives we'll ride him again.
> Oh, poor old horse!
>
> For a month a rotten life we've led,
> And we say so! And we hope so
> While you've lain in your feather bed.
> Oh, poor old horse!
>
> But now that month is up, old Turk,
> And we say so! And we hope so
> Get up, you swine, and look for work.
> Oh, poor old horse!

Get up, you swine, and look for graft,
And we say so! And we hope so
While we lays on, and yanks you aft.
Oh, poor old horse!

And after work and sore abuse,
And we say so! And we hope so
We'll salt you down for sailor's use.
Oh, poor old horse!

He's as dead as a nail in the lamproom door,
And we say so! And we hope so
And he won't come hazing us no more.
Oh, poor old horse!

We'll hoist him up to the main yardarm,
And we say so! And we hope so
And drop him down to the bottom of the sea.
Oh, poor old horse!

We'll sink him down with a long, long roll,
And we say so! And we hope so
Dover sharks 'll have his body, and the devil have his soul!
Oh, poor old horse!

I thought I heard the Old Man say,
And we say so! And we hope so
Just one more pull and then belay!
Oh, poor old horse!

CAPTAIN CHARLEY
Step aside, step aside and give me space,
you need medicine in this place
I am a rover just in to Dover...
Captain Charley is my name.
I have powders and potions which by my notions
I have fetched from distant shore.
I have sailed round Hope and Horn to Calibar... Malibar... and Zanzibar...
There... wonders I have found.
So now for Joey I will cure him with this bottle,

> I will drench him down his throttle…

Joey drinks potion and springs back to life.

> So now poor Dobbin lying here
> I'll bring him back and you will cheer…
> Even louder I suppose,
> when I powder off his nose
> So come on Dobbin don't be mort…
> I will shake if you will snort…

The powder is shook all over horse, that revives and looks perky but calm

> And now we need a smaller rider
> and one not full of Kentish cider.

Girl comes forward

> I have my daughter from over the sea
> and the champion jockey she will be
> Now here my lassie, don't be shy,
> come and give this 'orse a try
> Up to three now we all count,
> and on the horse's back you'll mount

ALTOGETHER LOUDLY
> ONE …TWO …THREE

Rider smartly gets on the back of the very obliging horse and rides about

MOLLY
> Huzzah, Hurrah, the day is won,
> our horse that we thought dead and done,
> has risen up with vigour new, and with easy rider can now walk, trot, canter,
> gallop and leap a five-bar gate.
> So now to bring our play to end…
> a song we'll sing and money spend
> on pork pie and Kentish beer.
> Good Christmas all and a happy new year.

Song

    Captain, Captain you are a Dandy
    Way Hey Shiny O
    Captain, Captain we love your brandy
    Way Hey Shiny O
    Won't you ferry me over to Dover
    From Calais the blue sea over

    Captain, Captain how deep is the water?
    It measures one inch six feet and a quarter
    Captain, Captain I love your daughter
    I want to kiss her and she says I oughter

    Shiny O is the Captain's daughter
    Just for her I'd sail across the water

    White horses they are running over
    When she pitches, she pitches into Dover
    Captain, Captain you are a dandy
    Captain, Captain we love your brandy

Autohoodening

As performed at Folkestone Folk Week 2022
Characters:
Alexis – Molly – Swing – Picker
Dash Macdonald / James Frost / Demitrios Kargotis / Nick Mortimer

Locate place to perform. Molly sets up position with speaker close by – Molly starts music. Swing/Alexis/Picker march around Molly for 1–2 mins in mechanical style. Molly stops / fades music – all others freeze in position.

MOLLY

>Welcome! Vroom Vroom! Give me vroom to Beep
>I'm Molly bot, sent here to speak,
>Of a tale from Amazon's machine of consumerism
>About workers and their treatment which is overdue some criticism
>
>All day long I see pickers' feet
>All day long we meet and meet.
>Unlike them I never get tired
>but they're in danger of getting fired.
>
>I've found humans asleep on their feet from working 55-hour weeks – BEEP BEEP
>We're living life as a cog
>hit your numbers or you'll lose your job.

Picker unfreezes and steps forwards.

PICKER

>In comes I, an exhausted picker. This evil scanner is forcing me to work quicker and quicker.

Alexis unfreezes and replies whilst snapping.

ALEXIS

>PICK QUICK! PICK QUICK!
>PICK, PACK, SNAP, SNAP
>
>your rates are down

speed up, speed up, speed up
speed up, speed up, speed up

Alexis chases Picker around Molly and both deliver lines.

PICKER
I have nightmares of not hitting the target rate,
If I don't work faster, I'll be out of the gate.

ALEXIS
Here at Amazon, we don't tolerate slow fools,
For I am Alexis the Scanner, and "the almighty rate rules!"

Hahahahahah

Pick, Quick, Pick, Quick!
Pack, pack, pick up the slack!
Snap, Snap, Snap

Swing shouts out – chase and Picker / Alexis freeze.

CAPTAIN SWING
STOP!

In comes I – Captain Swing,
against injustice I sing!
Forged through histories rebellion
Now armed and ready I rise again

I'm back to send these despots packing,
with a bit of system hacking.
Technology should not only profit the few
my bugs are ready to reprogram you.

Swing reaches into tool box to collect bug on stick

This is the bug of compassion,
corporate greed it will refashion.
What other bugs can we spread,
to end this misery and dread?

Picker unfreezes and takes a bug from the tool box triumphantly.

PICKER
> I will release this bug of trust,
> Constant worker surveillance is unjust.

Swing / Picker circle Molly once whilst dangling bugs towards her.

MOLLY [MOVES BACK A FEW STEPS]
> Please don't!
> Don't forget when you shop online
> The feel-good savings of money and time!

Swing / Picker thrust bugs into Molly – who takes them inside her. Molly shakes whilst feeling the emancipatory code seep into her digital veins.

MOLLY
> Proceed to b,b,b,basket
> perhaps not...
> It's time just words came from this bot.
>
> I recommend extra breaks and higher wages
> We're in the 21st century, not the dark ages!

Alexis unfreezes angry at Molly being tampered with.

ALEXIS
> Stop stop – you don't mean these things you say!
> I'll try a reboot, make this nonsense go away!
>
> How dare you think you can take me down?
> You'll look like a clown!
> My Molly will come back
> Forever you all will pack!
>
> Ahahahahah

Alexis chases Picker and Swing once around Molly; chase stops when Picker speaks.

PICKER
>They say they can simply replace us

CAPTAIN SWING
>So you must teach them your status.

PICKER
>I've had enough, this job is a trap

CAPTAIN SWING
>With this tape gun, the scanner we'll wrap

Swing and Picker chase Alexis with tape guns once around Molly and then wrap Alexis with ribbon. Alexis falls to his knees. Picker then inserts SD card into Alexis.

PICKER
>No longer will you torture us
>With mindless hours picking stuff.
>Once your sim card is replaced
>This world will be a more equal place!

Swing moves towards Alexis and pats him on the head.

CAPTAIN SWING
>At last you'll have no choice
>You will listen to our voice!

Alexis awakes and speaks as a changed horse.

ALEXIS
>Error Error 5, 4, 3
>
>*Time Off* ... Resist until ... *free time* ... is mandatory ... stop exploiting ... target greed ...

CAPTAIN SWING
>Now Alexis works for you

Alexis gets to his feet.

PICKER
>Our voice is strong
>Our tasks are few

ALL TOGETHER
>The power's back in worker's hands
>Give us our rights, hear our demands!

Molly starts music again and all take a bow.

ABOUT THE AUTHOR

James Frost is a freelance curator, artist, designer and puppeteer, with experience in outdoor theatre and folk drama practices such as mumming and hoodening. He works to commission in set design, prop, puppet and mask making.

He teaches classes in theatre design at Canterbury Christ Church University. He is a visiting lecturer in design at Goldsmiths, University of London, and Birmingham City University. He has published and presented academic papers on animal guising, puppetry, animation and the history of tarot cards.

He is a trustee for In A Space arts charity, and co-founder and Chair of the community arts and heritage group Bringing Alive Sandwich Heritage.

https://www.jamesedwardfrost.com/

ŌZARU BOOKS

Ōzaru Books is a boutique publisher based in the Thanet village of St Nicholas-at-Wade. Our primary focus is on books with a local connection, ranging from creative writing by East Kent authors to (occasionally niche) scholarly tomes about Kentish history, but we have a secondary interest in works in translation, particularly from Eastern languages, and also tales from East Prussia. Some of our profits go to support gorilla charities, which is the origin of the name Ōzaru ('Great Ape'). Two of our publications particularly concerned with Hoodening are shown below.

Discordant Comicals – The Hooden Horse of East Kent
George Frampton ISBN: 978–0-9559219–7-3

"a good read for the layman as well as a valuable resource for anyone interested in the custom" (The Morris Dancer)
"very readable research [...] reveals a tale of rich cultural heritage." (The Living Tradition)
"well presented [...] previously un-published interviews [...] in depth analysis [...] extremely interesting" (Around Kent Folk)
"the most up-to-date and comprehensive starting point for any scholar interested" (The Journal of Folklore Research)
"Frampton has left no stone unturned in his research [...] there is a very useful index, which helps make this a book to dip into profitably" (Archæologia Cantiana)
"admirable spadework and academic endeavour" (Master Mummers)
"a treat for the eyes [...] meticulous & detailed [...] compelling and intriguing" (Tykes' News)

The Hooden Horse of East Kent – Annotated Edition
Percy Maylam *Available on Kindle*

This eBook includes the whole of Maylam's text, with features to help those wanting to push the research further – copious annotations, internal hyperlinks, images of and external links to original sources, and appendices with contemporary reviews. The eBook naturally allows readers to search the whole text, yet the page numbers are still present to enable cross-referencing to Frampton and others. The list of subscribers is present, along with brief biographical notes, to show who was reading Maylam and what impact he would have had at the time.

www.ingramcontent.com/pod-product-compliance
Lightning Source LLC
Chambersburg PA
CBHW042259280426
43661CB00098BA/1194